Roberto Timo

RHODES

The Queen of the Mediterranean and the Wall Street of its Era

411 B.C. – 44 A.D.:
the splendor of a Maritime Republic,
1500 years before Venice

Out of the swirling sea came forth

an island, held by the father of the sharp rays,

ruler of the fire-breathing horses;

lying there with the nymph Rhodes he got

seven sons, who showed the wisest minds among men of old,

and of these one got Camirus, Ialysus, the eldest, and Lindus;

apart from one another they held,

with the land of their father divided in three,

their share of cities, their abodes being named after themselves.

Pindar, Olympian Odes VII, 69-71:
To Diagoras of Rhodes, boxer

The Author

Born in Aosta in 1961, he graduated in Economics in Torino in 1983.

He worked in merchant banks, in the international consulting firm *Bain* and, finally, as a self-employed professional, mainly as an expert in corporate finance. Among the professional positions held, he has been a long-standing member of the board of statutory auditors of the Italian bank *UniCredit.*

In Italy, he established *Callan, Timo e Associati,* a joint venture with the world leader in financial consulting for pension funds.

He is the author of many technical publications on topics mainly of finance, control systems and pension funds.

He directed the technical magazine *La Rivista dei Fondi Pensione* and, together with Gianfilippo Cuneo, he wrote the book on pension funds *Come funzionano i Fondi Pensione.*

Today, he resides in Luxembourg, where he is a member of the board of directors of several asset management companies and private equity funds.

Table of Contents

List of maps

List of Illustrations

Preface

The Maritime Republic of Rhodes – What have Wall Street and Venice to do with it? – The reasons for a book – The facts I propose to recount – Just one footnote

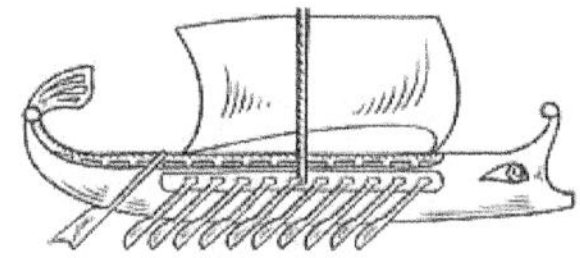

The Maritime Republic of Rhodes

In 411 B.C. or a few years earlier, some men had an extraordinary idea: to make Rhodes the centre of global trade in grain.

Grain: the major food in the ancient world, in its importance more or less the strategic equivalent of oil today.

Global: the world known to the Greeks, the Mediterranean Basin and the adjoining lands.

Rhodes: a strip of land with up until then a relatively marginal place in Greek history.

These men not only had a brilliant idea but also knew how to implement it. They constructed a port, in fact five, in strategic locations; they also constructed a city and surrounded it with a mighty wall. They built a fleet which, from the perspective of that time, was at the forefront in terms both of ship-building technology and seamanship capacity.

They plied the seas and, besides grain, carried many other goods.

They became a financial force, the 'Wall Street' of their times. They gave themselves a 'democratic' constitution, but in reality a few families always held power, although without abandoning concern for the common good, in this way ensuring consensus and avoiding the expense of internecine strife.

Their diplomacy played a major role in resolving the conflicts of the age. The law of the sea they drew up is in essence that which we still use today. The city was not only 'opulent' but also 'splendid', one of the beacons of civilization of those days: it attracted and exported the greatest artists, architects, orators, technicians and military geniuses.

And all this lasted for a good four and a half centuries. The aim of this book is to narrate this story.

What have Wall Street and Venice to do with it?

The title of this book is: Rhodes, the Queen of the Mediterranean and the Wall Street of its Age – From 411 B.C. to 44 A.D... The Splendour of a Maritime Republic, 1500 years before Venice.

The reason for the reference to Wall Street will become evident from this account of events in ancient Rhodes: both were (in the case of Rhodes) or are (in the case of Wall Street) the principal financial centres of their age.

But what is the point of the reference to the place which many centuries later will be the most famous maritime republic in history? Is it just a way of making the title of the book more attractive

In my view, no; the parallels with the future Venice are impressive.

It is difficult to sum up the essence of Venice in a few lines, but I will try. At the outset, a community restricted by nature to the edge of the sea might have remained a marginal group of fishermen with limited economic activity. Instead an entrepreneurial spirit prevailed.

Men of substance and adventurers plied the Mediterranean routes, dealing in all goods but above all dominating the flow of imports from the Orient to Europe, primarily in spices.

They constructed ships at the forefront of technology; for a long time, the shipyard of Venice was the biggest workshop of the world. They dominated the seas, not least thanks to the abilities of their seafarers.

On the basis of commerce, they created an important financial centre.

Their diplomatic skills allowed them to survive larger neighbours.

A limited number of families always wielded power, but the availability of great riches to distribute and the vision to do so always prevented internal divisions, both political and social. They built a splendid city which was also one of the great poles of culture of the time.

When external circumstances, the discovery of America and the replacement of the previous weak Byzantine Empire by the Ottoman Empire meant a lethal blow to its 'business model', it still managed to survive for three centuries.

Yes, it became slowly poorer but was still capable of maintaining its independence and splendours: its great urban architecture did not die with the discovery of America and the majestic manors of its hinterland all followed those events.

Venice experienced three centuries of decline before Napoleon closed it down, but it was a decline which created and provided a home to artists such as Bellini, Tintoretto and Tiepolo; and then there were also Carlo Goldoni, Ugo Foscolo and how many more besides? Thus, it remained until the end a beacon in the culture of its epoch.

I do not wish to anticipate the contents of this volume too much; to describe them is the task of the chapters that follow, but I would ask those who will read this book to the end to share with me whether they think that the idea of parallel histories between Rhodes and Venice is a figment of my imagination or is based on real facts - despite the gap of a millennium and a half!

The reasons for a book

Why did I, who am not a professional historian, decide to write this book? Quite simply because it had yet to be written.

Let me tell you in a few lines how it happened, because that too is part of the fascination of Rhodes.

About ten years ago I started to visit the island, for the obvious reason of spending my summer holidays there. I knew, like all of us, that in the Hellenistic era it had been one of the most important cities of the Mediterranean, but not much else, and I wanted to find out more. However, I have never found anything that got to the heart of the subject.

Practically nothing has been written about Hellenistic Rhodes. There are many studies and books about Rhodes during the period of the Knights of Saint John (1305-1523) and even more about the years of the Italian occupation and the Second World War (1912-1945), but the silence about the years in which Rhodes competed with Athens to be the most important city in Greece, the Hellenistic period, is deafening.

After endless searches I found a volume, the translation into Greek, commendably sponsored by the Chamber of Commerce of Rhodes, of an English book Rhodes in the Hellenistic Age.

The author is Richard Berthold, a professor of Ancient History at the University of New Mexico, who, on his retirement, published it in 1984. It amounts to a painstaking work of rereading dozens of 'classical authors' (Polybius, Vitruvius, Titus Livy and many more: practically all of them had written about some event concerning Rhodes).

Berthold's book is a most thorough work: a tour de force of information gathered, to which my work owes a lot, in particular because of its list of events and their chronology.

However, it never became a best-seller, probably because, having put the enumeration of facts before a continuous narrative, the work is not easy to read. I have every sympathy with Berthold who never visited Rhodes in his life and whom I never met personally. I try to imagine the old philologist immersed in reading hundreds of classical texts noting all the references to Rhodes and then reordering them to create an exact chronology.

It is because the historical representation of Rhodes owes so much to Berthold that this book opens with an expression of homage to him.

At the beginning of the volume I have placed a verse from one of Pindar's odes (the seventh of the Olympic odes). It is the same one as the American philologist uses to open his book. Moreover, it is obviously an act of homage to Rhodes, 'the daughter of the sun' and 'bride of the sun'.

Nevertheless, my aim is different.

It is to write the story of Rhodes at its zenith in an accessible style. Years ago, I read a book entitled The Egypt of the Pharaohs written by Federico Arborio Mella in just such a style. I was struck by the Introduction.

The author explains that after a visit to the Valley of the Nile he wanted to increase his knowledge of classical Egypt but could not find any suitable book. There were either very superficial accounts or academic tomes aimed at experts in the field. He therefore decided to write personally something that would be interesting to read.

As a dilettante historian, I have tried to take up the challenge in relation to Rhodes.

The focus of this book is not on individual events or on the names of various Navarchs (that is to say admirals), or other successions of personalities, given that Rhodes at that time was the fruit of collective efforts. Rather, the book will deal with the distinctive character of this project and on how Rhodes had to deal with the international context with which it was confronted.

I have tried to shed light on how this island, geographically off the beaten tracks and until then occupying a somewhat marginal role in Greek history, was able to become in the Hellenistic age a strong and prosperous maritime republic, which dominated commerce in the Mediterranean, and to be a prototype for what was to happen, a millennium and a half later, in Venice and Genoa.

As regards Berthold, an important element of added value I should like to provide is that of singling out and describing the characteristic foundations of this maritime republic.

I have also attempted to present, as best as I can, events which are not strictly political or military, whereas, on the basis of the American research, most authors have tended to focus their attention on the political and military dimensions. Rhodes in the Hellenistic Age, purged of some details, forms the narrative skeleton of my text, whilst totally new are the history of the period before 411 B.C., the analysis of the fundamental characteristics of the maritime republic, the references to later history, as well as the references to archaeological discoveries and to the economic, artistic and cultural life of Rhodes at that time.

At the end of the book I have included a note on bibliographical sources.

The facts I propose to recount

I think the above suffices by way of preface. Now I will move on to the narrative.

These are the titles of the chapters:
a-what, from myth to history, happened on the island before the construction of the city of Rhodes. In history, breaks in continuity are rare: even a phenomenon which seemingly emerges from nothing almost always represents the resurgence of a river from an existing underground flow;
b-how Rhodes (411-323) created the conditions to be able to flourish in the third century;
c-the fundamental and distinctive characteristics of The Maritime Republic of Rhodes;
d-the events of the 130 glorious years (323-188);
e-the dignified and obstinate, but never dull, long decline (188 B.C.-44 A.D.)

Just one footnote

One final notice: this book does not have footnotes. Some writers use them masterfully; I have Bulgakov's The Master and Margarita in mind. However, I also have in mind too many books where the footnotes are either entirely insignificant or an irksome distraction.

After due analysis of my conscience, I need to admit that I am not Bulgakov and accordingly, dear reader, I will spare you them.

Chapter One

The background: from the origins to 411 B.C.

The myth – The first inhabitants – The arrival of the Indo-Europeans and the Trojan War – The Dorian Hexapolis – The Economy of the Archaic World – The colonies of Rhodes: Gela and the others – The predominance of Lindos and the cult of Athena Lindia – Agrigento – The great men of the archaic period: Cleobulus 'the sage', Diagoras 'the pugilist' and the others – Events on Rhodes in the context of Greek history

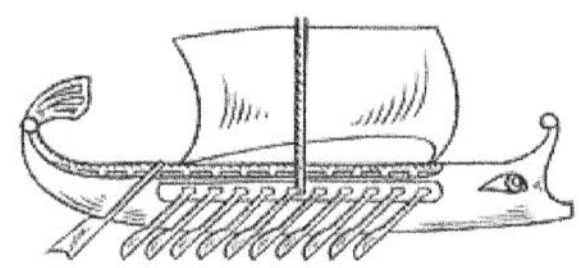

The myth

A Greek myth tells that one day Zeus summoned the gods and divided the earth among them. However, Apollo was absent, hunting. When he returned, he was not pleased to have been excluded from this partition. This created a problem for Zeus, Apollo not being a minor god easily silenced, yet at the same time Zeus could not go back on anything he had already assigned to the others.

It was a good thing for him that he was a god or rather the king of the gods. He caused a new land to emerge from the sea, the island of Rhodes. The god Apollo immediately repaired there with his chariot drawn by four horses of fire. And it was love at first sight between the god of the sun and the mountain surrounded by sea.

From then on Rhodes was always the 'Bride of the Sun'; whoever doubts this should go there, even in winter, and he will immediately understand why the oldest religion of the island was the cult of a sun god.

Is this really the truth? Of course not: not only because it is a myth but also because the Greeks/Mycenaeans brought the worship of Apollo to Rhodes only when they arrived there in approximately 1500 B.C., when man had already been present on the island for millennia and the cult of the sun god had already become firmly established.

The importance of sun worship on Rhodes needs to be underlined. The sun god was a largely marginal divinity, if he existed at all, in the Greek and Aegean region. On the other hand, he was central in the Egyptian world where the god of the sun Ra was the king of the gods. This bears witness, in the specific field of religion, to the bridging role Rhodes had from the outset between the Hellenic/Aegean and the Egyptian world.

As a matter of fact, the Mycenaeans incorporated the previous local cults into their own theology, identifying the sun god with Apollo 'Helios', which simply means sun.

From then on, Apollo would always be the protective god of the island and the most venerated. Various major temples would be dedicated to him and above all, the celebrated statue, one of the seven wonders of the Ancient World, known as the Colossus of Rhodes. We will return to this later.

Let me just add that bronze bulls dedicated to the sun god still existed in the classical era, but they had been made much earlier. They were placed on Atavíros, the highest peak of the island at above 1200 meters. The particular feature of these bulls was to have specially placed cavities through which on windy days, that is to say almost always, they bellowed down from on high to pay homage to their god. Then, at the same place, the Indo-Europeans built an altar to Zeus and then later the Christians built a church, a sign of the changing cultural times.

The first inhabitants

Moving from mythology to history, or rather pre-history, it is known that Anatolia (the modern Turkey) was one, or even the most, important place where a concentration of human population gathered following the discovery of agriculture and the domestication of animals.

We are talking of the period around 10,000 B.C.. From Anatolia humans progressively colonized the Mediterranean from east to west, initiating the flux of population known to historians as the 'Cycladic Expansion'. It is highly likely that Rhodes, just a few miles from the Anatolian coast, was among the first territories to experience human presence – perhaps only intermittently at the beginning.

The first certain proof of human presence on Rhodes dates from 5,200 B.C. and consists of remains from some excavations near Ialyssos, exhibited today in the Archaeological Museum of Rhodes.

However, an indirect earlier proof can be deduced from the presence of the Rhodian deer, one of the symbols of the island. They are native animals, a few hundred of them, who, having lived a long time in isolation, have developed into a distinct species in accordance with the well-known process of 'island dwarfism'. This differentiation seems to be the result of an isolation going back to 10,000 B.C.. However, at that date the island was already sufficiently distant from the continent to make it impossible for the ancestors of today's deer to swim so far. And so? The most rational and fascinating explanation is that they were brought by humans in the Paleolithic Age, in order to have wild animals to hunt.

Leaving aside such speculations, it is certain that from 5,000 B.C. Rhodes had a stable population. Moreover, we already encounter a feature of the later Rhodes, a substantial concord among its inhabitants. This is indirectly confirmed by the fact that its settlements were not surrounded by walls, a feature which stands out in comparison with the imposing megalithic walls that characterize the neighbouring territories of Greece, other Aegean islands and Anatolia.

The arrival of the Indo-Europeans and the Trojan War

Around 1,700 B.C. a new population arrived from Crete, the Telchines. The closeness of the two islands has always meant that there has been significant cultural and demographic exchange. Around 1,500 B.C. the first people speaking an Indo-European tongue, 'Greek', arrived, the Mycenaeans. From that point on, the history of Rhodes substantially resembles that of the rest of Greece.

We have a historical memoir of that period thanks to Homer, who, in his 'catalogue of ships' (Iliad, Book II) informs us that Rhodes participated in the Trojan War with nine ships commanded by King Tlepolemus, the 'Heraclides' (son of Hercules).

The number of ships gives us an indirect insight into the relative importance of Rhodes in the Mycenaean world: modest. There are only nine Rhodian ships mentioned out of the complete list of 1186 in the Iliad, that is to say only a few in comparison with the hundred ships of Mycenae and Tyrins commanded by Agamemnon, the eighty from Crete and even the thirty launched jointly by the other two great Dodecanese islands, Kos and Karpathos, together with the tiny Kasos and Nisyros and commanded by two men called Fidippus and Antiphos.

For those interested in mythology I add two anecdotes.

The first, taken from the Iliad, is that Tlepolemos died after being pierced in the throat by Sarpedon, the leader of the Lycians, whom he had challenged to a duel. This is the myth but when we come to the historical narrative, we shall see that the enmity with Lycia was a constant factor for Rhodes.

The second, a juicier one, is that the pierced king left behind a widow, Polyxo, who after his death reigned over Rhodes. The Homeric epic was also followed by other traditional stories following on from the fall of Troy. One of these claims that the Greeks, having found Helen in burning Troy, wanted to kill her as punishment for her infidelity, which had caused the war. At the critical moment, however, her former husband Menelaus arrived. Helen then uncovered her breasts to show him her undiminished beauty and he, once more enamoured, protected her and carried her back to Sparta.

However, on the death of Menelaus, Helen became aware of all the hostility surrounding her. At this point, Polyxo intervened by professing great friendship and inviting her to Rhodes for protection. Her intention, however, was different. Polyxo hated Helen, blaming her for the death of her beloved Tlepolemos and the invitation was a trap. According to tradition, the famously beautiful Helen committed suicide by hanging herself on a tree on Rhodes to avoid greater shame.

The Dorian Hexapolis

With the collapse of Mycenaean civilization around 1,200 B.C. Rhodes, like the rest of Greece, descended into a period of darkness known as the 'Greek Dark Ages'. The Greek world re-joined history in the eighth century, the time of Homer and Hesiod, the same also of the first stable Hellenic presence in the western Mediterranean.

The Island of Rhodes
The three original cities and their territories
Future city of Rhodes
Ialyssos
Kamiros
Lindos

With the 'return to history', we find Rhodes stably inserted into the 'Dorian' world together with Crete and above all Peloponnese of Sparta and thus in opposition to 'Ionian' Greece, the great champion of which was Athens.

In the eighth century, Rhodes re-emerged from the mists of the Greek Dark Ages with three cities: the most important in this archaic era being Lindos, with its splendid natural harbour, which is still inhabited today. Then there was Ialyssos which, for those who know Rhodes, is by the sea some ten kilometres away from today's city of Rhodes, and finally Kamiros, the smallest one, the ruins of which can be visited today on the west coast.

The three cities divided the island among them and were allies in a Dorian confederation, which also included Kos island, Knidos (abandoned today and located on the nearby Turkish peninsula of the same name) and Halicarnassus, today's Bodrum on the Anatolian mainland.

As with all the Greek leagues and confederations, the Dorian Hexapolis had a shared place of worship where presumably the treasure of the league was also stored. Such a temple was located at Cape Triopion, today's Cape Krio, not far from ancient Knidos. Here games also took place periodically, in honour of Apollo, obviously, but also of Poseidon, the god of the sea. The reason why the favour of this god was also sought is easy to understand.

Dorian Hexapolis and the territories belonging to Rhodes

The Economy of the Archaic World

What might the economy of Rhodes have looked like during these centuries?

As in all the ancient world agriculture will have been king, and here Rhodes will have been no exception.

Topographically, the island is still the same as created by Zeus: a mountain that emerges from the sea, steep on the west side and more level but also more arid to the east.

Judging from the centre of gravity of the location of the three main ancient settlements, the northern part was already richer and more populous than the southern one.

The terrain does not favour the cultivation of cereals, of which Rhodes was always an importer, but still nature has been generous with the island, endowing it with a mixture of soils and ready availability of water. Indeed, Rhodes is rich in water: the heavens drop around 60 centimetres of rain per year on London 'where it's always raining', whereas on Rhodes 'where it never rains' there are around 100 centimetres per year. The trick is not to get caught in the open on those days when the waters descend and truly pour down beneficially filling the aquifers and making possible the existence of springs and streams which never dry up, even in the hot summer. All of this is not bad, for a location south of Tunis!

This climate has always allowed the cultivation of what have always been the principal local products: grapes, figs, olives and vegetables. On the mountains, besides deer, even in ancient times tens of thousands of semi-wild goats will have roamed.

Fish have always been a scarce resource. Few rivers flow in the southern Aegean and thus the organic matter carried by them is scarce and does not provide enough of the first link in the food chain necessary for fish. Another factor is that Rhodes's continental shelf, especially on the eastern side, slopes very rapidly and there are few platforms at limited depth, of the kind essential for the growth of the newly born fish, the 'fry'.

Rhodes had a strong artisanal tradition, with the ceramics from Kamiros standing out. Vases manufactured there from the eighth century onwards have been discovered in various Mediterranean locations. There are those who claim that even the famous 'Nestor's Cup' with its scenes from the Iliad originates from Kamiros. It is one of the best conserved Greek artefacts of the eighth century and the pride of the museum of the island of Ischia, at that time called 'Pithekoussai', which was the first Greek settlement in the western Mediterranean.

There is no shortage of timber on the island, but it is on the mountains of the interior from where it is difficult to transport. It is much easier to cut down the mighty trunks needed for building on the nearby Asian continent and drag them to Rhodes, pulled by boats. Anatolia would always be the source of timber until recent times; there is no reason to believe that this was not the case from the earliest of times. The provision of long trunks, one of the strategic materials for shipbuilding, is one of the reasons for the importance of Peraea, the strip of coastal land in Anatolia opposite the island, the ownership of which Rhodes always considered strategic. I do not wish to get ahead of myself. I will talk about that in more detail later.

Obviously, Rhodes was also a place of small-scale trading. In the context of coastal daytime navigation, every island, almost up until today, was an important port of call. Only steamships, a century or so ago, would render them less essential, leading to economic crises on many Greek islands, which sometimes lost their whole *raison d'être*.

Nevertheless, Rhodes above all still needed trade to guarantee the supply of grain. It is not difficult to surmise that Egypt had been the main trading partner since the beginning, because it was the major granary of the time and it was also relatively close geographically. This explains the importance of Lindos, which was the leading city of the three on the island until the end of the fifth century B.C., as it was the only one with a natural harbour and coincidentally well situated for Egypt.

However, Rhodes certainly did not enjoy a 'rich' economy. This is proved both by the significant lack of monuments discovered on the island from the period up until the fifth century, and by the need to create new colonies for population.

The colonies of Rhodes: Gela and the others

Let us turn to this issue for a moment.

The Ancient Greeks founded colonies for various reasons: the creation of commercial hubs was one, with

Pithekoussai having already been mentioned, whilst the pan-Hellenic colony of Naukratis on the Nile delta provides another example. Another reason was the need for new settlements for citizens displaced from their own cities, following enemy conquest. There is also the case of Marseille founded by Phoenicians fleeing the Persians, whilst there might be other generically 'political' motives, as is the case with the Spartan city of Taranto.

However, the vast majority of Greek colonies were founded for reasons of overpopulation, a symptom of poverty rather than power.

Many colonies grew to become more opulent than the mother city, yet always remained linked to it. However, this should not make us forget that they came into existence because the mother city was no longer able to feed the growing population out of its own resources.

The phenomenon was not new. The process of migration from east to west was what populated the Mediterranean. Beginning in the Neolithic eras this 'Cycladic Expansion', which I have already referred to, was dictated by the necessity in every generation to transfer that part of the population which exceeded the growth in resources, away to new territories.

This progressive expansion of the population from east to west explains the substantial genetic uniformity of Mediterranean populations from Anatolia to the Iberian Peninsula.

None of this is anything to be surprised about. The need for a group of citizens to emigrate in search of territory is a phenomenon which has endured almost up until our own times. The European colonization of the Americas concluded no more than a century ago (just think of the trail to the Far West), and it was nothing more than the need for new territory on the part of European nations. These had become overpopulated and had to send many of their sons to areas which offered as yet unexploited resources, that is to say the Americas.

Let us return to Rhodes and the time under discussion. The Rhodians created some colonies on the nearby Lycian coast. The most important was Phaselis, but there were also the settlements of Gage, Coridalla and Rhodiopolis. Together with Knidos, they founded the colony of Lipari in the west, off the coast of Sicily. They participated, this time entirely for economic reasons rather than because of overpopulation, in the pan-Hellenic hub of Naukratis in Egypt.

On the other hand, the idea that Roses (Rhode, in Greek) on the Spanish coast north of Barcelona might have been a colony of Rhodes is disputed and appears to have been discounted by most historians. The only indication is the name.

The queen of the Rhodian colonies was, however, Gela. In 688, forty-five years after the Corinthians had founded Syracuse, a group of inhabitants of Lindos, guided by a leader called Antifamos and accompanied by a group of Cretans from Heraklion led by a certain Eutimos, founded on the south coast of Sicily the colony of Gela, which was one of the most important of 'Magna Graecia'.

Lindos played a central role in this adventure, but it is probable that other Rhodians participated in the initiative. Nevertheless, it is certain that the leading city of the island was the driving force. Moreover, although the initiative was a joint venture involving Rhodians and Cretans, it was the former who provided the leadership. This is attested by Thucydides who tells us, 'The men of Lindos had already been there' and, above all, there is the proof based on the fact that Gela's most important god, the one to whom the principal temple of the Acropolis was dedicated, was Athena 'Lindia'.

The predominance of Lindos and the cult of Athena Lindia

Let us devote a moment to this divinity, in the religious life of Rhodes second only to Apollo Helios.

Lindos, suffering from an arid climate, enjoyed however a most favourable geographical location: an apron of land above the sea, reaching up to an altitude of 116 meters and surrounded to the north and the south by two splendid natural harbours.

It goes without saying that it played host to a human presence from the time of the first human settlement on the island, a presence which in fact has been proven through archaeology to date from the Neolithic Age.

Those inhabitants had their own protective goddess, a *spiritus loci*, one of those 'mother goddesses' which were so important in the religions of all the eastern Mediterranean before the arrival of the Indo-Europeans.

When they arrived, in the middle of the second millennium B.C., the Greeks identified in accordance with their syncretic practices the goddess of Lindos with Athena, that is to say Athena 'Lindia'. This is no more and no less than the way they identified the primitive god of the sun with Apollo 'Helios'.

From the earliest origins of the city until the end of the pagan world with the arrival of Christianity, the cult of the goddess on the acropolis of Lindos remained most important.

The Acropolis of Lindos

In the earliest times on the acropolis there was probably only a sacred wood, but soon a temple was constructed, which in the middle of the sixth century under the governorship of Cleobulus was rebuilt more grandly and beautifully. It was a temple built on steps and placed on the edge of the site, to impress as much as possible whoever was approaching the city.

The temple of Athena at Lindos was the first large temple on the island of Rhodes. Destroyed by fire in 340 B.C., it was immediately reconstructed even more splendidly, but was destroyed definitively – as ever a fire was to blame – at the beginning of the Christian era.

Since then we have lost it forever thanks to neglect and earthquakes. The *coup de grâce* was when, in the fifteenth century, the knights of St John built one of their coastal defence fortifications on the remaining ruins. Since the beginning of the twentieth century, the acropolis has been the object of archaeological excavations, firstly by Danes, then by Italians between the two world wars and today by Greeks.

However, very little remains, and it is almost impossible for visitors with untrained eyes even to imagine the signs of ancient splendour.

Agrigento

Let us return to events in the colony of Gela. In 582 B.C., a hundred years after their arrival, the Geleans founded Akragas, today's Agrigento.

Akragas was to become, after Syracuse, the richest, most important and most populous Greek city in Sicily.

Thus, if Gela is the daughter of Rhodes, Agrigento is the grandchild, and a lot of Lindian blood flowed there.

Today Agrigento is famous throughout the world primarily for its Greek temples of the sixth and the fifth centuries B.C., the 'Valley of the Temples'. Designated a UNESCO world heritage site, they are very well preserved.

Agrigento - The Temple of Concordia

None of them are dedicated to Athena Lindia: none ever was, or possibly in the course of history one may have been re-consecrated or renamed?

In any case, with the disappearance of the temple of Athena in Lindos and with the temples of Apollo on Rhodes (of which we will speak separately below) suffering the same fate, and the ancient temple of Athena Lindia in Gela being in an abject condition, all that remains for us are the great temples of Agrigento with their pure Doric style and their mighty imposing splendour.

To have a 'visual' idea of what the great temples of Rhodes were like, I would maintain that we should look to the grand temple of Concordia at

Agrigento and try to transfer it in our imagination to the razed locations of the acropolises of Rhodes and Lindos, rather than to look at the few miserable stones which archaeologists have worthily brought to light on the island.

The great men of the archaic period: Cleobulus 'the sage', Diagoras 'the pugilist' and the others

Another topic: the great men in the archaic era of Rhodes who have not been forgotten by history.

The first in chronological order is Cleobulus of Lindos. He reigned over the main city of the island for forty long years in the middle part of the sixth century. We have already come across him as the builder of the great temple dedicated to Athena. He was numbered among the seven sages of antiquity, on the same level of great characters as Thales and Solon. In reality we know little about him, the most extensive but still sketchy information coming from Diogenes Laërtius.

The thinking of Cleobulus, on the evidence of the aphorisms quoted below, is based on the philosophy of moderation: 'The best thing is moderation'; 'Listen much and speak little'; 'Overcome pleasure'; 'Do nothing in a spirit of violence' and so forth – recommendations that remain relevant today. We also know that he was a man of great beauty, as we can judge from the homosexual eulogies he received from the poet Anachreon. It is also possible that he was the promoter of the first currency on Rhodes, which would come to play a fundamental role in the story of the island and in the financial history of all the Hellenic world, as we shall see.

The other shining light of archaic Rhodes was Diagoras of Ialyssos. I should record that Pindar's Seventh Olympic Ode quoted at the beginning of this work is dedicated to him. It is known that Pindar was a great sycophant who, in order to make both ends meet, sought out the great, or rather the powerful, patrons of his time. But who was Diagoras of Rhodes (or rather, at the time, of Ialyssos)?

Born of a noble Dorian family, he won the Olympics for boxing in 464, an achievement for which a statue on Olympia was dedicated to him and specifically Pindar's ode. Subsequently a soothsayer predicted that he would die on the happiest day of his life.

A generation later in a subsequent Olympiad, three of his sons (Damagelos, Akusilaos and Dorieus) all won on the same day the competitions in boxing, pankration and wrestling. On their return to Rhodes, acclaimed by the crowds, two of the three champions lifted their father, who had preceded them in glory, onto their shoulders, carrying him in triumph in front of the cheering crowds. It was thus that 'on the happiest day of his life', in triumph on the shoulders of his sons and in front of all the people of Rhodes, the great Diagoras died suddenly (because of his intense emotion?).

Another important figure of the age was the epic poet Pisander of Kamiros, who lived at the time of Cleobulus and was the author of the *Heracleia*, two volumes dedicated to the labours of Hercules.

Rhodes - The monument to Diagoras

He was probably the first author to represent the mythical hero covered by a lion skin and with a club in his hand. The great glory of Pisander came posthumously when in the third century B.C. the editors of the Alexandrine Canon of Epic Poets put him in third place after two great poets of the calibre of Homer and Hesiod.

Another son of the island was the lyric poet of the fifth century Timocreon. We know almost nothing about him. Expelled from Ialyssos for political reasons and having arrived in Athens, he tried to attach himself to the bandwagon of Themistocles but, having been snubbed, he turned against him, making him the target of particularly venomous verses.

Events on Rhodes in the context of Greek history

Let us now try to put all the preceding narrative in its context, within the 'History' (this with a capital letter) of Greece.

To sum up: Rhodes was inhabited from the Neolithic Age onwards by people of Anatolian descent and from the outset there were important links with Egypt.

Like the rest of Greece, it was conquered by the Mycenaeans in the first half of the second millennium and, at the time of the Trojan War, it was indeed allied to the other Achaeans but did not stand out for its significance. It then disappears from historical narrative, again like the rest of Greece, in the four centuries of the Greek Dark Ages. When it re-emerged in the eighth century, Rhodes was securely positioned in the Dorian, as opposed to the Ionian world.

At the beginning of the fifth century there was a momentous change in the history, not just of Greece but perhaps of the whole of humanity, a change which is also marked by the passage from 'Archaic' to 'Classical' Greece.

The Persian emperor Darius, determined to punish Athens for the support given to the rebel Ionian cities, dispatched an army. It was the year 490 B.C. and Athens, left on its own by the other Greek cities with the exception of the small Platea, managed to defy the troops of the 'king of kings' at Marathon. It was a heroic feat, even if the outcome appears explicable by the fact that the Persians had only sent a fraction of their forces.

It was not to be the same outcome some ten years later in 480, when the new emperor Xerxes arrived in Greece with all his armed forces. This time the threat was mortal and all the Greek *poleis* united. The first to be massacred were the 300 Spartans of Leonidas at the Battle of Thermopolis, but it was the naval battle on 23 September at Salamina that proved decisive. Here the Greek fleet under the command of Athens, and in particular thanks to Themistocles, decisively defeated the enemy, thus liberating Greece forever from the nightmare of submission to Persia.

Rhodes, too, was involved in the Battle of Salamina with forty ships but… on the wrong side: that of the Persians. In addition to the possible opportunism of the moment, this seems to me a further undeniable proof of a somewhat weak sense of belonging to the Greek world on the part of Rhodes at that time.

It goes without saying that the victorious Athenians did not take things well and took revenge in the area where, even then, the pain caused has always been the worst for the Rhodians: the wallet.

Rhodes suffered a period of hypertaxation with only brief periods of relief now and then when Athens, for reasons of foreign policy, could not afford rebellions by its vassals.

Unfortunately for itself, Athens adopted this rapacious imperialistic approach in confrontations with all the Greek cities, and this put an end to the most splendid fifty-year period in the history of the city.

In 431, still in the time of Pericles, some cities rebelled and united with Sparta, giving rise to the Greek civil war known as the Peloponnesian War, which only finally concluded in 404 with the defeat of Athens.

Rhodes, led by the 'democratic' party, that is to say the pro-Athenian faction, remained faithful to Athens for a long time, however always seeking to limit to the minimum its exposure and expenses.

However, the situation changed in 411 when, following a small naval victory of the Spartans at nearby Symi, the party of the 'oligarchs' led by Dorieus, son of Diagoras, with the support of the Spartans ousted the 'democratic' government and took power at Ialyssos.

Thus in 411 Rhodes changed sides and became an ally of Sparta. However, above all, this was the momentous year in which there began the triumphal march, which later would make Rhodes the 'Queen of the Mediterranean'.

411 A.D. is the symbolic date which the core of the story in this book takes as its point of departure.

Chapter Two

Preparation: from 411 to 323 B.C.

A strategic intuition – The choice of location for the new city – The ports – The 'new' city and Hippodamus –The walls – The centrality of the city in relation to the island – Political events of the fourth century – The great Rhodians of the fourth century – Lysippos and the bronze horses – Alexander the Great dies

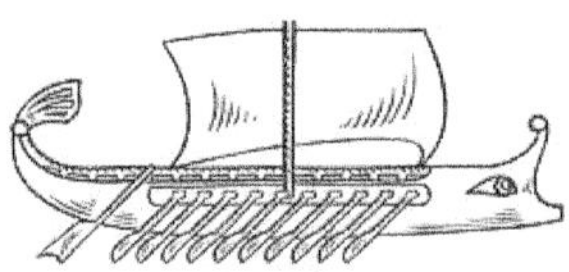

A strategic intuition

Let us imagine a surreal scene, but one which might help us to get over the idea.

The year is 411 B.C., we are on the island of Rhodes, possibly at Ialyssos, and a board meeting is taking place according to today's rules. A group of men of authority, wearing tunics rather than jackets and ties in view of the date, is sitting around a meeting table.

The company is Rhodes plc, the body that manages the economy of the island. The directors are drawn from the most prominent families of each of the three cities. In the chair is Dorieus, the former winner of an Olympic contest and the head of the Diagorides family, which has just assumed power in Ialyssos. The agenda contains just one item: the strategic plan.

Dorieus hands over to a consultant who starts his presentation consisting of large panels which are attached to the wall one by one by servants, slides projected onto a big screen not having been invented at that time. The room is in semi-darkness in order not to divert attention away from the walls where the panels are attached, which by contrast are well lit. The board members listen in silence and take some notes, engraving waxed tablets with their styli.

The first panel displays the economic situation of the island, as we too examined it in the preceding chapter: surplus of luxury products such as wine and oil but shortage of grain, which renders trade with Egypt essential, competitive in artisanal products, good supply of wood and so on.

This amounts to a Greek economic reality shared with many others, basically in good shape although subject to taxes imposed by militarily stronger actors.

The economy of Rhodes, however, is burdened by strategic risk, as the men around the table know well, namely that one unfavourable event could unleash the 'great plague' of Greece: population growth greater than that of its economic resources, followed by the inevitable and painful emigration of many of its sons.

The 'great plague' of today's Greece was not so different two and a half millennia ago. This is the reason why that morning these men have come together to think about a strategic plan on which to base stable economic growth for the economy of the island.

The consultant does not speak much about the first panel; the facts are known to those present.

He passes on to the second panel: the importance of grain, the staple food for the ancient world of the Mediterranean. An obvious point: the members of the board are beginning to wonder whether the celebrated strategy consultant has just presented this panel to fill up some space. It is well-known that consultants are paid according to the number of pages!

The third panel has two colours. It shows the central and eastern Mediterranean. In the middle is the Aegean Sea, the heart around which the Greeks live as if in a ring. To the north are Macedonia and Chalkidiki, to the west the most important region, comprising Attica with Athens and Peloponnese with Sparta; to the south a barrier made up of three islands: Crete, little Karpathos and Rhodes itself. Finally, in the east there is the Anatolian coast, which, even if at that time subject to the Persian Empire, could not have been more Greek.

This ring was coloured red, the colour chosen by our consultant to indicate the shortage of grain. To the north and south of the central part of the map there are two green zones marking the grain exporters: to the south the valley of the Nile, the most important one, and to the north the coasts around the Black Sea, connected to the Aegean by the two straits of the Bosphorus and the Dardanelles. We are in 411 B.C.; the fact that other areas of the Mediterranean, principally Sicily, might later become exporters of grain was not yet known to these men.

The fourth panel is the same geographical map as before, but full of lines which cross the sea. These are the nautical routes which each polis or Greek island plies with their own ships to supply themselves with grain in exchange for their own products. The board members are beginning to look more interested. Even this was known to them, but one of the great skills of strategy consultants is that of focusing attention on known facts.

Eastern Mediterranean

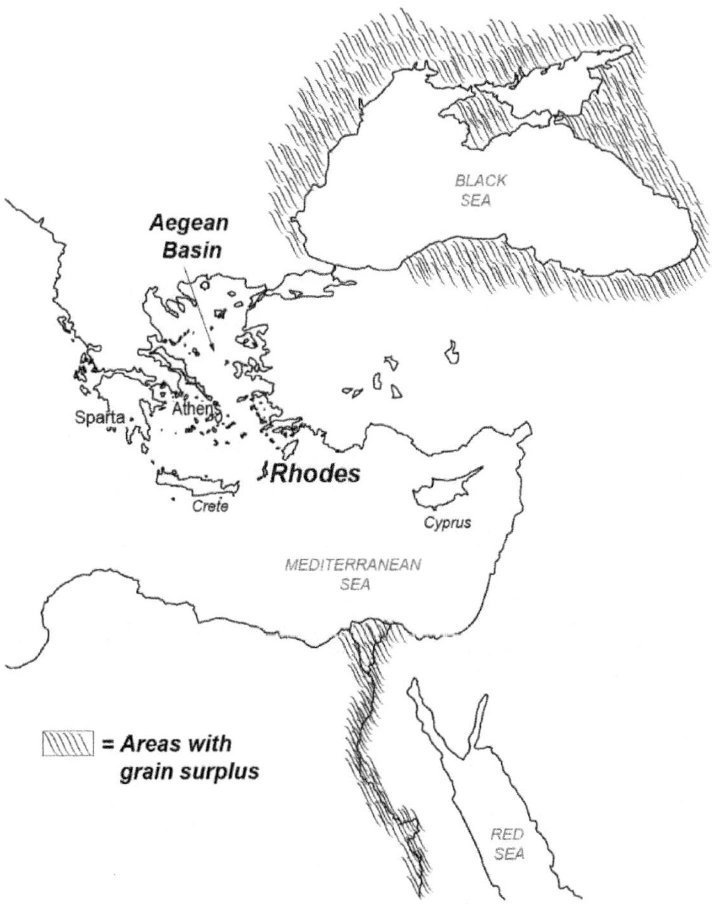

The fifth panel is once more the preceding geographic map, but the lines now marked are those of the prevailing winds in the Aegean. Why? Simple.

In ancient times sailing was restricted to the summer months and was by sail. Accordingly, the direction in which the winter winds blew was irrelevant, whilst the consideration that the summer winds blew down at great speed from north to south was highly relevant. When sailing, at the time, it was much easier to run with the wind; but to reload with grain Greek ships had primarily to 'head into the wind' from south to north to go toward the Black Sea. Of course: in order to stock up on grain the Greek ships had first to get to the Black Sea.

If 'heading into the wind' is still difficult today, we should note how difficult it was with the nautical techniques of those times, particularly the way ships were rigged. The aim of this panel was not to show the direction of the winds, which was generally the same, but their intensity. Those people today who hire a sailing boat for a holiday in the Aegean know that to sail towards the north on the central Cycladic route is unwise. The western route which runs near Athens and the Peloponnese is better, even if longer, and still better is the eastern route hugging the Anatolian coast. And it is exactly on this last route that Rhodes is situated.

The sixth panel is 'conceptual', covering 'economies of scale' in the grain trade and on the 'competitive advantage' of the island of Rhodes. The terms are high-flown. The directors stay silent; someone has understood what it is all about and this is the highlight of the day, whilst the others keep silent only not to look silly. Even in this respect two and a half thousand years have passed and, as I know from personal experience, meetings of boards of directors still follow the same pattern.

The 'economy of scale', in this specific case, consisted in replacing the variety of operators who every year sent their small boats northwards and southwards to obtain the supply of grain with the creation of a single or at least major centre, what today we would call a 'hub'.

Thus, the idea was to send from a single point impressive fleets to Egypt and the Black Sea carrying Aegean products, reloading with grain to sort and distribute for the whole Hellenic world. The 'competitive advantage' would fall to Rhodes, since it was, on the one hand, the polis of the Aegean closest to Egypt and, on the other, if certainly not the nearest to the Dardanelles, nevertheless part of the best route with the added advantage that it was also free of the Persian presence with its heavy taxation.

The brilliant solution and the strategic idea was to create a hub for the grain traffic of all Greece and establish it at Rhodes, which fulfilled all the preconditions for it.

Those present at the meeting felt enlightened, whilst remaining dumbstruck in admiration. Dorieus, too, pretended to be so. In reality, like all self-respecting company chairmen and CEOs, he already knew the conclusions of the celebrated consultant. Furthermore, to a large extent, he had dictated them to him.

The seventh panel only needed a fleeting glance. It consisted solely of a title 'Measures of Implementation'. Consultants love difficult words, being faithful to Kant's ironic adage: 'Be obscure, you will be considered profound'. This sounds like 'So what do we do?'. It is clearly a panel which the more and more illustrious consultant included only to add to the volume and hence to the bill, but at this point the directors let it pass.

The eighth panel is the explosive one: a) let us construct a port at the optimal place on the island; b) let us build a city behind it which acts as a market, and c) let us construct strong walls around it: nothing can attract an enemy better than a rich but feeble society.

Before the representatives from Lindos can see which way the wind is blowing and say something, there is a rapid change to the next panel, the ninth and last: where to put the new port and new city.

Everything is obvious: on the northern tip of the island; for those who know the conclusion of the debate, exactly where it is today. The situation is perfect; it offers more than a natural harbour, there is vast virgin land to construct a city, it is suitable for building defensive works. And it is better positioned than the current major port on the island: that of Lindos.

The facts are incontrovertible: on the route to Egypt, landing at Rhodes (city) or at Lindos makes almost no difference, whilst for all the other routes, the Aegean basin or the Black Sea, a base at Rhodes rather than Lindos saves every time almost a day's navigation by sail, almost two if you count both directions, which multiplied by the number of ships... an enormous quantity for anyone wanting to establish a logistics centre. And also, the position of the city would be better: Lindos is still most beautiful, that is to say a dream from a touristic point of view, but there is no drinking water, whereas on the other hand it is abundant at Rhodes: by default, where would you put a city with potentially tens of thousands of inhabitants?

The representatives from Lindos, caught on the back foot and almost totally unprepared, fight verbally with tooth and nail. Against them there are the men of Ialyssos. It's their idea, the new city is on their territory, they gave the consultant his cue (sorry, his briefing). Able to tip the scales in the dispute are the directors from Kamiros, the small city located on the rocky west coast and totally unsuitable for a port. Without having any personal interest to defend, they choose the common interest. The new city will be built: where it is today.

Did things really go like I have described? Obviously not. Did the Rhodians debate rationally and plan to become the grain hub for Greece? Who knows? But it's all irrelevant. Let me continue in a frivolous vein. Some years ago, Bill Sharpe won the Nobel prize for economics for his studies on financial asset management. More precisely, his principal contributions had been some mathematical models for evaluating the results of asset management. To those who objected that possibly his conclusions were different from the managers' original intentions, he responded, let me say it in my own words, 'if an animal looks like a duck, behaves like a duck and says quack, quack like a duck, for me it is a duck.'

It is of little importance whether these men, in 411 B.C., decided scientifically to become the centre of the grain trade in the eastern Mediterranean, the 'world' of that time. What is certain is that they did so with a strategical coherence and an impressive ability to make it happen. So, think what you like, but for me it is a 'duck'.

To sum up: in 411 B.C., or thereabouts, somebody had a strategic intuition that 'made a difference', namely to convert an island of arid agriculture with some access to the sea into a well organised commercial centre, the 'Maritime Republic', which held sway the Mediterranean for four and a half centuries.

The choice of location for the new city

Now, let us examine in greater detail what those men built.

They chose a flat area in the northernmost part of the island, protected to the north and the east by the sea and to the west by the steep slopes of Mount St Stephen or Mount Smith, as it is called today. Incidentally, why rename what for centuries was Mount St Stephen? It is an act of homage to a British admiral, not even one of the most prominent ones, who lived at the time of the Napoleonic Wars and only made a fleeting visit to Rhodes. It seems to me an act of unjustified cultural subordination.

Allow me therefore the quirk of calling it from now on Mount St Stephen, that is to say with the traditional Rhodian name, which is also much more 'Mediterranean'.

However, after this diversion into the realm of toponomy, let us return to the pre-selected area, which offers so many natural recesses, perfect for installing ports and with so much fresh water available from wells. Moreover, as I have already intimated, it is in a location, perfect for the routes of navigation by sail, be it southwards towards Egypt or northwards towards the Aegean Basin and the Dardanelles.

No traces have been found here of previous settlements. In truth this remains *sub judice*, it is not easy to excavate in a city inhabited without interruption for more than 2400 years.

The ports

Here they built a port, in fact, whilst they were at it, they built five so that they faced all the geographical directions. Constant pounding by the winds and the sea, not to mention human activity, have altered the coastline over many centuries, so that the ports of that time were not exactly where they are today, but in general the differences are minor.

The main port is the middle one of Colona, and it has always been so subsequently. It is open to the east and from the beginning it has been enclosed internally by walls, whilst the mouth of the port was sealed with a chain. This port was largely devoted to the merchant fleet. Behind it arose the main shipyard, where ships were put on dry land in winter for maintenance; today, the offices of the electricity company Dei can be found here. Considering that in winter in this area there was a large concentration of sailors and workmen as well as the temple of Aphrodite, the goddess of love, it is easy for us to imagine which other profession flourished at this place in the ancient city of Rhodes.

Not much further south, almost a twin to Colona, there was a second port in the Bay of Acandia, where today the large ferries and the cruise ships moor. To the north of Colona and open to the north, was the port of Mandraki, where in the Italian era two columns with the deer of Rhodes and the wolf of Rome were placed at the entry. The wolf was replaced with a doe after the Second World War, for obvious political reasons. The Mandraki is also the place where some romantic traveller in the nineteenth century imagined that the Colossus stood tall. It was also called the ‘small’ port in contrast with the ‘big’ Colona one, and its purpose was primarily military.

The fourth port was more to the south and obviously open to the south in Zefiro Bay: on leaving the city it is shortly before you reach the modern cemetery.

The fifth port, the one to the west, no longer exists. It was more or less where today the square known as Hundred Palms is located. It was basically a kind of internal lagoon with a narrow entrance to the sea. The actions of the sea over many centuries and land reclamation to clear the marshy terrain during the Italian era have definitively consigned it to the land.

The ‘new’ city and Hippodamus

Behind the ports arose the city, ‘new’ at that time but today called the ‘old city’, in Greek ‘Palià Pòli’.

And here the Rhodians did not do things by half. They did not call in just a star architect, but The (with capital ‘t’) star architect of the time: the urbanist Hippodamus of Miletus. He had earned his spurs in the reconstruction, after the devastation caused by the Persians, of his native Miletus, was a veteran of nothing less than the construction of Piraeus, the port of Athens, a commission bestowed on him by Pericles.

Like all the great artists, he was not only a technician within his field, but also a visionary. His objective was the ideal city, regular and ordered in its forms, with streets rigorously perpendicular to each other and oriented north-south and east-west, with rectangular blocks, *insulae* of around 16 by 26 metres, and socially regulated with districts well separated among the three classes of artisans, farmers and soldiers.

The ideal city also had a maximum number of inhabitants: no more than 10,000. It is possible that this was also the initial size of Rhodes when it was planned. It only became a metropolis later, on the wings of its own success.

Rhodes was built between 408 and 405 B.C.. It is thought that Hippodamus died in 408. Thus, he had time to design his final masterpiece but not to see it completed. Nevertheless, his stamp is clear not only in the original intersections at right angles of the streets but also in the tripartite division of the city in accordance with its social classes.

To the north, on the highest point within the current medieval walls there were the public buildings, both civil, where today the palace of the Grand Master is situated, and religious, that is to say the first temple of Apollo Helios, where today there is the Turkish school, opposite the Grand Master's palace.

Around these it can be assumed that there were the palaces of the most prosperous families. Indeed, this will always be the role of the area throughout the centuries.

The primitive temple of Apollo Helios was replaced a century later by the great statue of the god, the Colossus.

In the Byzantine era, the area where the rulers lived, known as Collachio, was surrounded by a second encircling wall inside the main walls and today still partially stands.

The Knights of St John, when they arrived in Rhodes at the beginning of the fourteenth century, built the Grand Master's Palace on the site of the civil public buildings of the Diagorides era; the Cathedral of St John the Baptist was built where the first temple of Apollo Helios once stood.

Then they built, still inside Collachio, 'the houses of languages', that is to say the seats of the fighting units: the soldiers for whom Hippodamus had designed this district. Here the great hospital was also built, an inescapable obligation for a military order with an 'hospitalier' mission.

And furthermore: when the Ottoman sultan Suleiman entered Rhodes after the siege of 1522, he established the first mosque, praying to Allah in St John's Cathedral.

The cathedral was automatically converted into a mosque by his particular prayer. Then he provided the funds so that the first true discrete mosque could be quickly built alongside, which is still called the 'Suleiman'.

Time passed, there was a later occupation, that of the Italians, but the seat of power stayed at the same place: immediately after reconstruction the Grand Master's Palace became the seat of the Italian viceroys.

Slightly further south is the commercial quarter. We are also close to the internal port and next to the gates of the city, leading to Acandia and Mandraki. And this will also always remain the commercial zone as, for example, the grandiose warehouses of the medieval merchants of the Italian maritime republics underline. Even today the quarter is crossed by the main shopping streets (Socrates street and, leading down, Aristotle street), which are unfortunately also teeming with sellers of tasteless junk for tourists and tiresome characters who approach passers-by to lure them inside bars and restaurants.

Finally, to the south there is the largest part of the city, the working-class district, inhabited from time immemorial by artisans and workers. Today it may have fewer architectural attractions, but it is a place which is worth wandering around for tourists, because it is more authentic.

The island of Rhodes is very prone to earthquakes. Hippodamus went to great pains to exploit all the earthquake-proof technology known in his time: houses no higher than two storeys, the lightest possible roofs so as to limit the injuries to the unfortunates who might be underneath if they fell, a vaulted arch on the ground floor, still present in a good number of the houses in the old city and having the purpose of reinforcing the building, as well as a perpendicular arch at first floor level between two houses, so that each building supports the other. For those going through the alleys it is only necessary for them to raise their heads, to see numerous examples of this.

Anti-seismic Arches in the old town

The building material is obviously local stone, a sandstone extracted from the quarries at Kalithea, located a few kilometres to the south east of the city by the sea, and thus easily transportable by raft.

The walls

After the ports and the city: the walls.

Planned to be imposing, the walls were the main defence of the city and the network of ports.

First question: which areas did they enclose?

To make the explanation simpler let us begin with looking at the medieval fortifications, which still exist. Those of the original city had the same footprint in the east, alongside the sea. To the north, the ancient walls, constructed to protect the port of Mandraki, lay beyond the medieval ones. They reached the sea more or less opposite today's Main Post Office. To the south, excavations have identified them at the same location as the church of St Francis, that is to say the same position of the medieval ones as well. Where the original city extended further to the west, here they extended as far as the ridge of Mount St Stephen, including the main part of the Acropolis.

The walls were not built in one day: once completed on the basis of Hippodamus' design, they were re-assessed and modified several times in the fourth century B.C., principally because the city was flooded three times. The final flood, in 316, almost caused the collapse of the wall. For this reason, major subterranean drainage works were carried out; even though they have not yet been brought fully to light, they have made a great impression on archaeologists.

Finally, something for those who like historical snippets: from the very first days the burial and industrial zones were located outside the walls, both to the south, where they still remain today. It would not have made sense to put them elsewhere. To the east there was the sea, to the west the ground climbed steeply, whilst the small amount of open space to the north was swampy.

Today the old burial zone has become accessible for history fans, thanks to archaeological excavations, whilst the industrial one is supposed to have been underneath the recently closed factories to the south east of the city towards Zefiros Beach.

The present building of the CAIR, the wine-making company founded by the Italian government, the mill, a candy factory, these closed as well, and other former industrial buildings stand where in ancient times one could find the ceramics workshops, the tanneries, the joineries, the blacksmiths' forges... This was a logical choice; since such places produced smoke, noise and bad odours, what could be better than to place them outside the city, near the sea and downwind?

The ports, city and wall completed, Rhodes was ready for the Great Adventure. I do not wish to anticipate anything that happened next, preferring to recount it comprehensively in the next chapter.

The centrality of the city in relation to the island

What is essential to stress is that, with Rhodes constructed between 408 and 405, from then on the history of the island becomes forever that of the city.

In fact, the inhabitants of Ialyssos moved to the new city, and the modern town does not retain any traces of the ancient times. Kamiros loses its lustre before being finally abandoned after the earthquake of 142 B.C.. Only Lindos has found a way of carrying on, but this beautiful little town no longer had a position of leadership in the succeeding great events.

Political events of the fourth century

Let us consider now the political events which marked Rhodes from the foundation of the city until fateful 323, the year of the death of Alexander the Great, marking for historians the start of the 'Hellenistic period' and, as far as we are concerned, the real independence of Rhodes.

The supremacy of the Diagorides only lasted around fifteen years; in 396 power returned to the Democratic party led by Dorimachus. Not all the details of this event are known, but a particularly convincing hypothesis is that there was in reality a kind of agreement between the two factions, the democratic and the oligarchic. The following facts would support this hypothesis: very few of the Diagorides and their supporters were killed or sent into exile; b) from then on the two factions lived in peace and harmony; c) Dorieus, leader of the Diagorides, as the reader knows, went to Sparta asking for asylum but he was executed there. A vendetta? Certainly, but why kill one of one's own side fallen into misfortune? Doesn't it in fact appear more likely that the Spartans believed that Rhodes had simply changed sides in the international alliances and that the mission of Dorieus was just play acting with a view to try to 'maintain relations' with them as well?

What is certain is that the main consequence of the shift in power at home was precisely the change of alliances. Rhodes, for fifteen years the 'friend' of Sparta, moved to the side of 'democratic' Athens. Sparta did not have the time to react; two years later, in 394, at the Battle of Cnidus, the Persians destroyed its fleet once and for all.

At this point it is necessary to place events in Rhodes in the broader context of those in Greece as a whole. Sparta in 404 ended the struggle with Athens by winning the Peloponnesian War. However, as early as 401, it became involved in the war of succession in Persia which opposed Cyrus the Younger against Artaxerxes II. Misfortune had it that Sparta supported the losing side; we know of these events thanks to the *Anabasis* of Xenophon.

From 394, with the fleet destroyed by the Persians in the above-mentioned Battle of Cnidus, Sparta's supremacy wavered, and some twenty years of conflicts reignited among the Greek cities, which seemed to come to an end only in 371 (Battle of Leuctra) with the supremacy of Thebes. That however proved an illusion. Greece's internal wars continued until 338, when Philip II of Macedonia subjugated the whole country after the decisive Battle of Chaeronea. His son, Alexander the Great, in 334 then set out to conquer the Persian Empire and only his untimely death in 323 stopped his advance.

The first ninety years of the history of the Maritime Republic of Rhodes, those that I have called 'the age of preparation', can be placed within the framework of these events.

The individual battles, alliances, temporary periods of supremacy, seen from a historical perspective, today only appear a monotonous and not very relevant succession of episodes of subordination to the strongest power of the moment. It is almost irrelevant, on the basis of today's knowledge, to know what happened, to whom and when.

Now it was Persia, now Athens. In 357, when Rhodes rebelled against Athens with Kos, Chios and Byzantium with the support of Mausolus of Caria, an 'Aegean League' was created.

There followed the supremacy of Caria and then that of Thebes. Finally, Philip II subjugated the whole of Greece and Rhodes, too, became a tributary of Macedonia.

To sum up in a few words: what was relevant at this time was not politics but the expansion of the commercial routes, the improvements to the fleet and the city fortifications: this was, in broad terms, 'the age of preparation'.

Nevertheless, it was a very advanced 'preparation': still in Alexander the Great's lifetime, his governor of Egypt, Cleomenes, had already recognized Rhodes as the wholesale market and the redistribution point for the grain produced in the valley of the Nile.

The great Rhodians of the fourth century

Dorieus stands out above all others. We have already talked about him. We do not need many words to underline that he was the greatest, the true "father of the Fatherland", the one who caused Rhodes to become what it became.

However, at this time, in Rhodes there was no shortage of other important figures; in the world of arts let us remember Antiphanes, Anaxandrides and Dinocrates, Rhodians who made their fortunes elsewhere, and Lysippos, one of the most important sculptors of his age who, by contrast, also worked on Rhodes.

The first two left their native Rhodes (to be more precise Anaxandrides came from Kamiros) for Athens, where both were the major interpreters of the literary genre known as 'Middle Comedy'. 'Middle' has only a time-related meaning: it flourished from the eighties of the fourth century until the time of Philip II of Macedonia, in the 'middle' between the 'old' comedy (e.g. Aristophanes) and the modern (e.g. Menander). Unfortunately, no complete work has survived from that period. However, we do know that everyday life interpreted by stereotypical characters was the main subject of this kind of comedy, rather than politics, together with parody of mythology, the same mythology that provided the material for the tragedies of Euripides. Great attention was also devoted to more escapist subjects, primarily the seduction of virgins.

Both Antiphanes and Anaxandrides enjoyed great public success; it is known that the latter was repeatedly awarded with the Oscar prize equivalents of the time: the Dionysia, the Lenaia and even an Olympiad.

The architect Dinocrates, however, was the proof that Rhodians were learning fast. We have seen how Hippodamus designed Rhodes. Some eighty years later Alexander the Great wanted to build a city to symbolise his glory, which would have been the capital of his empire, if death had not cut him down in his prime: Alexandria in Egypt.

The emperor devoted a lot of energy to the project; he personally chose the site, its dimensions, the placing of the monuments, the road network and the orientation, considering the salubriousness of the air. The sovereign, as we know from Vitruvius, wanted a city with secure ports and an emphasis on commerce, by both sea and river. And he wanted it designed in accordance with Hippodamus' philosophy. Dinocrates of Rhodes, aided by the other architects Cleomenes of Naucratis and Crates of Olynthus, was the one who built it for him.

Alexandria was the main achievement of Dinocrates, but not the only one: he was responsible for numerous works in the sacred cities of Delphi and Delos, he created the monumental tomb of the Macedonian general Hephaestion and he took on the delicate task of restoring the Temple of Artemis at Ephesus, one of the seven wonders of the ancient world.

This architectural interchange with Alexandria, part of larger and constant exchanges between Rhodes and Egypt, did not finish with Dinocrates. After the earthquake of 228 B.C. we find the Alexandrian architect Amphilochus very involved in the reconstruction of Rhodes.

Military geniuses were not lacking among the great Rhodians of the time: the brothers Mentor and Memnon, as mercenaries, were the principal generals of Persia at that time. The elder, Mentor, reconquered Egypt on behalf of the 'Great King'.

The younger Memnon, commander of the western army of the shah Darius III, facing the attack of Alexander the Great, suggested to his own sovereign a strategic retreat in order to extend the lines of supply of the enemy: that is to say a 'scorched earth' policy. I imagine it to have been something similar to that executed masterfully many centuries later by Marshal Kutuzov, enticing Napoleon's army into the heart of Russia and destroying it by exhaustion more than by force of arms.

Darius did not follow Memnon's advice, accepted the challenge and was defeated at the Battle of the Granicus: the beginning of the end for the great Persian emperor. If the Great King had listened to Memnon, would the outcome have been different? Who knows? History is not made up of 'ifs'.

However, I should like to point out that twenty-two centuries later, a new invading Greek army re-entered the fray on the same territory. It was the army of King Constantine and his prime minister Dimitris Gounaris.

They wanted to recapture western Anatolia from a Turkey down on its knees after the Ottoman empire had been defeated in the First World War. The Turkish commander, Mustafa Kemal 'Ataturk', knew he was weaker and following the old lessons of Memnon and Kutuzov, created scorched earth and retreated and retreated. He accepted battle only after weeks against a Greek army with thinned out ranks and difficult supply lines. It was a disaster for the invaders, one of the greatest Greek tragedies of all times.

Lysippos and the bronze horses

Lysippos was a foreigner who spent some time in Rhodes, the first of a long series of important artists. He was probably the most important artist of the fourth century: a sculptor in marble and bronze as well as a painter. Students of the history of art would underline how his style is easily recognisable by its wiry, lean bodies and the great attention given to the subjects' hair. A historian, however, would emphasise the fact that he enjoyed great success whilst still alive. He was a friend of Aristotle and the official portraitist of Alexander the Great.

It is obvious that for the magnates and the civic authorities of the time it was a matter of prestige to commission works from him and he, who was well-paid, was not backward in offering his services.

Of his many works, the statues are particularly numerous, representations of victors, destined for Olympia, and the quadrigas donated to what was the most famous temple of Apollo, that of Delphi.

In this context the will to promote itself socially was at the heart of policy in the emerging city of Rhodes. It also called in Lysippos, who stayed on the island long enough to sculpt a giant quadriga destined to be given to Delphi. It represented the myth of Apollo (you may remember it) arriving on Rhodes to see his own island shortly after it emerged from the sea. In Delphi the statue was placed with the god facing west and thus with his shoulders to the east. It is the classic reference, indicating the sun which, every day, completes its course from east to west during the daylight hours.

I should like to devote a moment to this image of the chariot of the sun. It is a myth which does not form part, or only a marginal one, of Greek cultural tradition.

However, if you have visited the Valley of the Kings or just admired it on a photograph, you may have noticed the area to the west of the Nile at the same height of Thebes, where there is the highest density of the Pharaohs' graves. There, the chariot of the sun, which makes its way every day with its shoulders to the east, is an omnipresent motif. What the Rhodians commissioned from Lysippos and gave to Delphi was part of their more ancient culture with its roots in pre-Indo European times, something that was still very much alive in the fourth century.

This is further proof that Rhodes was a hinge between the Greek and the Egyptian world, not only in terms of commercial exchange but also in terms of culture: a much more permanent factor.

Furthermore, this cultural particularity of Rhodes had been well grasped by Aesop, who, already a century and a half earlier, wrote the fable *Hic Rhodus, hic salta*. What stands out in it is not the mockery of the braggarts, but the choice of Rhodes as an almost exotic place symbolising distance for those living in the heart of Greece.

Do you still want to admire this quadriga or at least get some idea of it? Then go to St Mark's Square in Venice (yet again Venice) and rest your gaze on the bronze horses which adorn the façade of the basilica. They were plundered by the Doge Enrico Dandolo in the context of the capture of Constantinople in 1204. In his turn Napoleon purloined them and took them to Paris. They were returned to Venice in 1815 and are one of the most celebrated monuments of the city by the lagoon.

We know that in Constantinople they were placed in the Hippodrome, and we also know that they were older. They were long considered to be a copy from the Roman era of horses from a quadriga by Lysippos. Previously they had arrived in Constantinople from an uncertain location (Chios? Olympia? Delphi?). Recent analyses by carbon dating have led the majority of experts to date them earlier and attribute them to the Hellenistic period and therefore consider them as an original work by Lysippos himself. Are they indeed the same horses casted on Rhodes or do they originate from a sister quadriga? Probably we shall never know, but they still offer us a fine visual representation of how much the artist produced at Rhodes.

The horses we can admire in St Mark's Square have also a particular technical characteristic: bronze is an alloy of copper and tin; the one used for the St Mark's horses has a very high percentage of copper, around 97 per cent.

That makes it shinier but also more expensive and difficult to work, a sign of an era of prosperity, as well as of not only great artistic but also of high technical skill on the part of the sculptor. I have underlined this aspect because we shall come back to it when talking of the Colossus.

The brief presence of Lysippos on Rhodes did not leave only the legacy of the quadriga, but above all a pupil who was to make a name for himself: Chares of Lindos.

Alexander the Great dies

Let us return to the subject of politics in the fourth century: all of a sudden, the time became ripe. In June 323 Alexander the Great died at Babylon and the people of Rhodes did not delay in putting the Macedonian garrison to flight.

Rhodes had finally added the last piece to the jigsaw: independence.

'The age of preparation' gave way to the 'days of glory'. However, before telling of the zenith of Rhodes, I think it is useful to describe the principal features of the Maritime Republic.

Chapter Three

The essence of the Maritime Republic of Rhodes

Grain – The 'World' of that time – The geostrategic location - The marketplace – The financial centre – Affluence – Naval supremacy - International maritime law – A metropolis and a capital of sciences and arts – Domestic policy – Foreign policy – The enemies of Rhodes – Control over Peraea and the southern Dodecanese – The walls of Rhodes and their story over the centuries

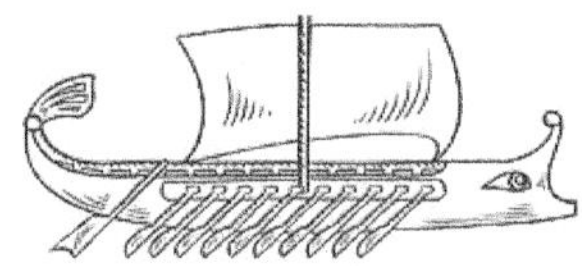

Grain

Let us set the zoom feature to maximum and try to capture the essence of Hellenistic Rhodes with a single word: GRAIN.

Yes, grain, the fundamental foodstuff in the ancient Mediterranean world.

In recent years two books have been extremely successful: *Salt: Grain of Life* by Pierre Laszlo and *Empire of Cotton* by Sven Beckert. They are both books which narrate the story of humanity in relation to such fundamental raw materials.

Many raw materials are important for man, but a limited number of these have been the key for survival and development; in addition to salt and cotton, one can think of coal and iron, in today's world oil of course, but not many others. Two, however, stand out above all the others because they are the basis of nutrition: grain and rice in the west and east respectively. It is strange that nobody, in the wake of Laszlo and Beckert, has tried to rewrite the story of humanity in relation to these two foodstuffs.

If we think about it, even today we feed ourselves with many different things which provide us with carbohydrates, proteins and fats and this has always been the case for ten thousand years from the beginning of the Neolithic Age, with grain and rice having been the basis of nutrition without interruption.

Their cultivation was a turning point in the history of humanity. The world changed from a place with a few million people, made up of semi-nomadic tribes of hunter-gatherers spread over the planet, to a world which, thanks to the better nutrition guaranteed by these two basic cereals, could support increased territorial concentration, develop specialist capacities and ultimately give a kick start to that process of cultural and demographic growth we call in short 'history'.

I maintain that capable authors have been able to write the story of man through the prism of salt and cotton. Perhaps someone will be able to write it through coal, iron and petroleum. It would not be easy to write it through grain and rice; it would be 'the universal history'!

The 'World' of that time

I hope that with the preceding brief comments I have managed to convey the importance of grain for the world in which ancient Rhodes found itself. I also maintain that it is useful to try to define what 'the world of that time' was like.

Above all, in the fifth century B.C., taking the planet as a whole, human beings did not number two hundred million, today we are more than seven billion: a ratio of around one to forty. Furthermore, entire continents, that is to say the Americas, Oceania, Europe, non-Mediterranean Africa and the largest part of Asia, were inhabited by small groups of people, who were still generally semi-nomadic.

Thus the number of human beings was not only small, but also concentrated in only three areas of the world: in China in the valleys of the Yellow and Blue Rivers thanks to the subsistence guaranteed by cultivation of rice, in India in the valleys of the Indus and the Ganges, again thanks to rice, and a 'Western World' delimited to the east by the Iranian uplands, to the north by the Black Sea, to the west by the Mediterranean and to the south by Egypt. And here grain was king.

The 'Western World', that among the three centres of demographic concentration which interest us, had as its centre of gravity the Aegean/eastern Mediterranean, which was bordered by the most important countries: Egypt, Mesopotamia, Palestine, Anatolia and Greece. The distant Iranian steppes to the east, and, to the west, Italy, where Etruscan and Tyrrhenian civilisations had already flourished and the star of Rome was beginning to rise, were its extreme limits.

Politically, the major part of this world belonged to the Persian Empire, with the conspicuous exception of the Greek world which had secured its independence at Salamina.

After that, within a few decades, all its parts had been united by Alexander the Great into a single entity: what we now call the 'Hellenistic world'.

In the previous chapter, I stressed that a handful of men in 411 determined to make Rhodes the major commercial centre for trading in grain in the Aegean basin.

If I have managed, in my preceding remarks, to convey to the reader that grain was 'THE' raw material and that the Aegean basin in terms of demography, economics, technical and intellectual supremacy carried, compared with the remainder of humanity, a superior weight than that possessed today by the United States, then I will also have conveyed the sense of how ambitious the project of these men of Rhodes was.

The geostrategic location

I explained in the previous chapter how Rhodes was very well positioned in the centre of gravity of the grain trade routes. I would now also like to examine its second biggest geographical advantage: being an island.

An island is easily defensible against external predators, especially if internally there are places that are easy to fortify, and because those who live there must necessarily own many ships to trade (or to make war, if necessary) while those who want to attack must acquire the ships, normally at a high price, to transport the troops required to achieve their purpose.

At the height of Venice's power, before the Battle of Lepanto, the arsenal was able to launch a galley a day; there was no other state that could do the same. In war, numerical supremacy has always been the key to having an often-decisive advantage. Possessing many ships also allows, if required, to make the troops necessary for the defence of the city move rapidly, even from distant places; the logistics for cities without a maritime tradition are not so easy.

For centuries it has been a great advantage to be a city-state located on an island in the centre of a wide and developing region accessible from the sea: it was the case with Venice (which consist of a complex of contiguous islands) and, in the Baltic, of the island of Gotland. Even cities located on coastlines protected by steep mountains, to give some examples, Amalfi and Genoa, were in a similar situation, because they were easily defensible against overland attacks and were unassailable if attacked from the sea.

The marketplace

First of all, I would like to say a few words to explain why having the 'hub' in the grain trade, i.e. the possibility of linking the Mediterranean areas that produced a surplus above the level of local consumption with those in deficit, gave Rhodes enormous leverage to profit from.

At the time, to defend themselves from pirates, ships often travelled in convoys, so the focus was on concentrating transport from areas of production to a single sorting point rather than from production point to final destinations (because in the second in case there would have been a greater number of routes to travel with single ships instead of in convoys).

This, incidentally, would also be the main reason for the existence of the Italian maritime republics a millennium and a half later.

Furthermore, in ancient times there was great variability in agricultural production between one country and another, not only because of the orographic and meteorological characteristics of each area, but also between one year and the next because irrigation systems were not much developed and therefore agriculture depended on the amount of rainfall. Consequently, if a population plants sufficient grain seeds to guarantee subsistence even when adverse weather conditions occur, it is inevitable that in most cases there is a crop in excess of needs, and this excess, in the absence of reliable transport, commands an extremely low value (i.e. price). Rhodes was always able to find grain surpluses in some Mediterranean coastal territory, transport them to its ports, and then sell them back to the deficit areas.

Buying a little and selling a lot has always been a simple but safe recipe for success; even other islands or states could do the same thing, but Rhodes had a central position, an orographic structure with five ports connected and easily defensible. It is therefore understandable that over time this competitive advantage concentrated the traffic on Rhodes.

Now let's get away from the grain and zoom out. Let us note: Rhodes dominated the grain trade in the Mediterranean, exporting it from the two main centres of production, Egypt and the area around the Black Sea, to all the consumer markets situated around the Aegean. This is the essence of the story; the rest is a matter of condition, consequence and complement. Let us examine them.

We have seen that everything started with a favourable geographic location, but one enhanced by the ports/city/walls system. However, this threesome neither contains the whole list of necessary instruments, nor does the slogan 'grain in the Aegean' encompass the variety of opportunities.

If you have ships plying the seas transporting grain and a system supporting it, it is obvious that you can trade and also make profits from many other goods. Thus, Rhodes took part in the slave, silver and wine trades (the latter being perhaps the only island product it paid to export) and in so many other markets.

If ships are transporting so many goods, besides the main routes they can open up many others. So, what originated in Rhodes could consistently reach the markets of the western Mediterranean. As early as 330 B.C., in one of his speeches, the Athenian rhetorician Lycurgus described the Rhodians as the cleverest of merchants.

The financial centre

Where there is an important market place, by definition, a financial centre also grows up. The phenomenon recurs throughout history. In the 1300s the first Florentine bankers were great merchant families such as the Bardi and the Peruzzi. All the Italian maritime republics were also financial centres. In English-language financial jargon, the word 'Lombard' still conjures up the old Lombard merchants who were also bankers in London. In modern times British leadership in the area of finance has its origins in the country's domination of the world of commerce; the British were part merchants, part bankers and part pirates.

History repeats itself, the process is logical.

Where goods change hands, money does as well; methods of payment for overseas trade (such as letters of credit, guarantees, insurance policies and the like) are necessary. Furthermore, it is only a short step from instrument of business to financial management, which becomes a lucrative business in itself. And so, to put it in plain words, Rhodes became the Wall Street and the City of its time.

I would add that a financial centre, to be successful, must enjoy the trust of savers, which means, first of all, physical security: the military defences of Rhodes were important, equivalent to the fact that today the political/military power of the two Anglo-Saxon countries is dominant. Then, legal protection: it is no coincidence that Rhodes - we will see - was a cradle of law and the parallel continues with today's USA and Great Britain that excel for legal certainty and defence of property rights. Finally, there is creditworthiness; today it is measured in the high scores from the rating agencies, at the time

Rhodes obtained it through its own seriousness in monetary policy.

Three episodes can help us to understand the importance of Rhodes as a financial centre.

Firstly: after Philip of Macedonia had conquered Greece, his son Alexander the Great sought to rationalise many things and, among other steps, imposed the standard Athenian currency throughout his empire. There was one exception: he also kept the Rhodian currency. This seems to me an important proof that Rhodes, although politically a subject of more powerful states, had already attained commercial power and, on that basis, financial power as early as 'the age of preparation'.

Rhodian coin

Secondly: after the devastating earthquake of 228, Rhodes was given financial aid from all the Mediterranean countries. This was also the case with politically hostile countries (except Pergamon, definitely too hostile), not to mention countries far poorer than Rhodes. A spontaneous act of naïve philanthropy? Hardly credible; disinterested generosity has never been a significant factor in politics in any era of history. It seems more likely that the entire Hellenistic world feared the collapse of the financial system which was based on Rhodes. Possibly, even then it was intuitively known that, by allowing Lehman Brothers to fail, the shock waves throughout the system would have been difficult to control and very costly for all.

Finally: in the last years of its history as a maritime republic, Rhodes had already substantially lost its independence and a good part of its former wealth. However, in 31 A.D., after the Battle of Actium, Rhodes made a different choice from that of almost all the other states subject to Rome. All were financially worn out from the devastation caused by decades of civil wars and, with the tacit agreement of Emperor Augustus, almost all declared themselves bankrupt. Rhodes did not. It preferred to honour entirely its own debts. Although paying an economic price for this, it maintained the greatest asset of a banker: confidence.

Affluence

Commerce plus finance equals: riches. Throughout the Hellenistic period Rhodes was the most affluent place in its world, even though it was far smaller than the three great monarchies (Macedonia, Syria and Egypt) among which Alexander's empire was divided.

Naval supremacy

A fundamental priority for a maritime republic is obviously control over the seas, something which can be guaranteed only by the effectiveness of its fleet. Clearly, Rhodes distinguished itself in this respect. This was not through the number or tonnage of its ships; how could an island compete in terms of size with the resources of empires by which it was confronted? It could do so by the quality of its shipyards and the skill of its sailors.

Concerning the quality of its shipbuilding, we have an indirect testimony when we read of the very strong pressure which Antigonus of Macedonia applied on Rhodes in the final years of the fourth century, to have military vessels built for him there. Not for free, mind you, but ready to pay through the nose!

Rather than large ships Rhodes had specialised in a particular type of quadrireme, a galley with four banks of oars, which stood out for its speed and manoeuvrability.

As far as crews were concerned, Rhodes made a fundamental, far-sighted choice. Its sailors were never slaves or mercenaries, but always citizens. Free men, 'owners of their own oar', people who were fighting for their own family and their own land and, it would appear to be a logical deduction, shared a part of the profits with the shipowners and the captains. Thus, it was frequently rich citizens, the 'trierarchs', who fitted out individual ships and small fleets, taking on all the costs, including the salaries, which were only subsequently reimbursed by the state. Does this not recall the large private fleets of the great families Doria, Spinola and others of the Republic of Genoa so many centuries later?

These, too, are recurring motifs throughout history; a millennium and a half later Venice dominated the Mediterranean, also using the technology of its own naval arsenal, a technological jewel of its day. Moreover, when in 1805 Nelson routed the French at Trafalgar despite having a smaller number of men, he could count, in addition to his own genius, on the greater individual professionalism of the English sailors compared with his adversaries.

International maritime law

International trade, finance and shipping need a law to govern them. One of the most lasting gifts which the Republic of Rhodes left to posterity is the corpus of navigation law. Today's international maritime law is still based on that of Rhodes.

It is perfectly reasonable to presume that in the community of men of the sea there were customary laws, but it was Rhodes that first codified them, with complexities and attention to detail, in its own maritime code, which established itself quickly thanks to the way it provided certainty in law. The Rhodian code of navigation, being 'international', could not be imposed, but was recognised universally as suitable to the requirements of a community that knows no national boundaries: that is to say, 'the international community of the men of the sea'.

When Rome conquered the known western world, the maritime law of Rhodes passed straight into Roman Law. Its significance can be seen from this extract from the laws of the emperor Antoninus Pius: 'these arguments are to be judged according to the maritime law of the Rhodians, unless one of our laws is (explicitly) contrary to it'. Equally, the laws of the Eastern Roman Empire or if you prefer, Byzantine, will be based on the Rhodian code of navigation: the code of Justinian of 534 A.D. incorporated a standard that was identical to the Roman one.

Nothing changed until the late Middle Ages, when it was felt necessary to recodify the laws of navigation, for example by the Amalfian Laws. Around 1200 A.D. three maritime codes were in force: The Book of the Consulate of the Sea of Barcelona for the Mediterranean, the laws of Oleron (after the eponymous French island) for France and England, as well as the Visby laws for the Baltic and the Hanseatic cities. Subsequently, with the power that came from its naval supremacy, England imposed Admiralty Law. However, all the norms laid down were nothing more than recodification of the ancient Rhodian Laws.

Still today it is the code of Rhodes that inspires the efforts to create uniformity at the global level, under the auspices of the International Maritime Committee created in 1897. It is true that large-scale intercontinental shipping, the tankers and the attention given to problems of major incidents of pollution, just to give some examples, have created new situations, but in its still relevant key provisions the basis of international maritime law is still that of the ancient Republic of Rhodes, for example concerning insurance, rescues at sea and partition of losses in the case of a shipwreck.

It is striking to think that, at two and a half millennia of distance, that any competent judge anywhere in the world seeking to determinate what happened, let us take an example, to a Japanese freighter off the coast of South Africa, is still applying ancient legal principles thought out by far off men from 'the bride of the sun'!

A metropolis and a capital of sciences and arts

Any important port obviously attracts people: merchants, sailors, artisans, adventurers.

The island that, not even two centuries previously, had been forced to send away a proportion if its own children, those that it could no longer afford to feed, to found colonies, had totally changed direction and had become a demographic magnet.

At the height of its glory, Rhodes was a metropolis by the standards of its time. The old city planned for a maximum of 10,000 inhabitants was accommodating more than 50,000; one estimate of the maximum number attained is 80,000. We are not talking small numbers. To provide some parameters: the world population had not attained two hundred million and the whole of classical Egypt always had around four million inhabitants, the Greek metropolis by definition,

Athens, might have had 300,000. Nevertheless, if the total number of inhabitants Rhodes managed to accommodate remains a matter of debate, one thing is certain: the number of foreigners and slaves outnumbered the natives; another significant proof of the strong force of attraction emanating from the prosperity of the island.

In their turn, new arrivals need homes and consumer goods and this stimulates economic growth.

A metropolis also attracts intellectual talents. Alongside the commercial city, Rhodes was to become one of the main poles of attraction for architects, artists, philosophers, students, technicians, astronomers, doctors and many others. We have already seen how Rhodes played host to a character such as Hippodamus and 'exported' Antiphanes, Anaxandrides and Dinocrates; this process of cultural exchange was to grow exponentially later. Rhodes attracted, to cite the most celebrated names, people like Apollonius of Rhodes, the young Cicero, the future emperor Tiberius and created, for example, some of the greatest artistic masterpieces of all times, notably the sculpture 'Nike of Samothracia', 'Laocoön and His Sons' and 'The Farnese Bull'. However, seeing that the zenith of Rhodes as a city of culture was to coincide with its time of political decline, I will postpone the account of it to that time.

Internal politics

Let us turn now to examining the features, unchanging during all its history, of politics in Rhodes.

In domestic politics, the fundamental constant of the Maritime Republic of Rhodes was the extraordinary cohesion. This is difficult to believe for those who know the island today or have studied events in ancient Greece. Nevertheless, it is true.

After the *coup d'état*, genuine or 'simulated', of 396 B.C., there were no more shockwaves in domestic politics and the episodes of dissent were also very limited.

Rhodes gave itself a democratic constitution; however, the government was in fact the prerogative of the great families. Was this cohesion due to an excellent constitutional system? From a layman's perspective, the constitution seems very similar to that of almost all the other 'democratic' cities (six-month appointments, political bodies with reciprocal checks and balances, and the like).

To describe it in a few words: the 'people' came together in an 'Assembly' at least twice a year to elect the two principal institutions, both for a period of six months, the 'Council' and the 'Prytanes'. The Council, the numbers of which are not known but whose members were salaried, pursued the task of representing the Assembly from day to day, whilst the five Prytanes, one of which was internally elected as president, functioned as the executive; in practice they were the government.

Obviously, with citizens who represented a minority of the population *in situ* (remember that the two groups, foreigners and slaves, were larger than that of citizens) and minors and women being excluded from the equation, those who enjoyed political rights were in reality few. If we consider further that many among the 'poor' sold their votes to the rich, as is recorded by an excellent witness from the Greece of that period, namely Plato, it is hardly surprising that power on Rhodes was always monopolized by the same few families, albeit under a democratic veil.

We know that, in the majority of the other Greek cities, this type of system, in essence always the same, did not prevent internecine strife. How come? What made a difference in the avoidance of political divisions was the availability of great wealth and the foresight of the rich to share out as much as was necessary to maintain social order.

Oscar Wilde wrote that rules are made for idiots, everybody else uses common sense. Personally, I agree and I am therefore led to believe that the ancient Rhodians, as clever businessmen, had an abundance of common sense. Nobody took his own interests or his own personal hatred so far as to create internal strife. Collective well-being, that is to say the 'size of the cake' was the most important objective for all. Then, when it came to divide, a sensible compromise was always achieved, both in the years of prosperity and, what is even more difficult, in the long years of decline. The consequence was amazing, especially if this is contrasted with the civil wars in the world of those years (Peloponnesian War, wars among the Hellenistic states, civil wars in Rome). Rhodes did not squander resources in internal strife and never gave foreigners a reason for intervening under the pretext of having been called in by one citizens' faction or another.

There is a thought that I would like to share with lovers of economic history. Rhodes was governed by an oligarchy, as would all the successive maritime republics be, clear examples of which are Venice and Genoa. Is there a link? Yes, in the nature of the business.

In a society based on maritime trade and finance, wealth is inevitably widespread, at least within an oligarchy. A king, who can easily be an owner and control wealth based on land, would not be able to control and be the owner of all the ships that travel the sea. Just imagine what would happen if every merchant ship, obviously expensive and very capitalized with goods in transit, was not owned by the ship-owning family, with one of its members present on board in each trip, and was instead owned only by the sovereign: for a crew of slaves or hired sailors the temptation to steal ship and cargo would be irresistible. Consequently, Rhodes and all the maritime republics had a political structure based on an oligarchy of wealthy families who controlled each other and not a king who owned everything.

Foreign policy

Neither distracted nor damaged by civil strife, Rhodes could therefore concentrate all its political energies on international events. Obviously, this was always systematically oriented towards safeguarding its own independence and increasing its wealth and power: in practice a foreign policy in support of commercial interests.

These, in schematic form, were the main thrusts of such a policy.

Search for peace. A merchant is hurt by situations of war. Accordingly, Rhodes made constant efforts not to become too involved in quarrels and to pursue compromise whenever possible, with the single proviso of safeguarding its own vital interests (we shall see that when we tell the story of the Great Siege of 305 B.C.). Rhodes always avoided involving itself up to the hilt, with the risk that an extreme choice could damage its own prospects of survival. Yet, its 'search for peace' and thus stability in the sphere of commerce also extended to conflicts between third countries. This is shown by the efforts Rhodes always made to act as mediator in disputes elsewhere.

A merchant must not antagonise its own customers. Rhodes therefore tried to be the friend of everybody, but always with an eye for particular sympathy for its own principal trading partner: Egypt. The description of this symbiotic relationship with Egypt deserves a few extra words. I have already described the cultural affinities which underpinned its roots in the furthest past.

The reasons why Rhodes carefully cultivated relations is obvious; if you are a trader, your main supplier is a most precious resource. However, let us seek to understand the advantages of this close relationship as well from the point of view of Egypt: it takes two to tango. Within the economic system of the ancient world, Egypt was extremely rich, with the fertile valley of the Nile allowing it to have a substantial surplus in grain. And riches allow one to have a strong army.

However, Ptolemaic Egypt, like that of the Pharaohs before, had a serious Achilles' heel. It possessed neither timber nor iron: the strategic materials for building up a fleet. Accordingly, Egypt had a strong army, but lacked an adequate navy, had an excess of products suitable for export but limited facilities within the maritime logistical system. Accordingly, Rhodes provided a complement; it had the fleet and a viable shipbuilding industry.

The marriage between Rhodes and Egypt functioned perfectly since it was based on common interests instead of love: Rhodes provided Egypt with a fleet and Egypt paid it back by allowing Rhodes a commercial rate of profit on its grain.

Safeguarding its own independence. By preventing the emergence of a single major power. Just like Britain did in Europe two thousand years later, Hellenistic Rhodes concentrated all its efforts in search of a balance of power.

Exactly when, at the beginning of the second century, with the predominance of Rome, this balance was reduced, the political autonomy of Rhodes was also reduced and with it also its prosperity.

Being the 'champion of the little states'. Either Aegean islands or small city states. Ensuring the existence of the small helped to maintain the balance of power.

Here, too, Rhodes paid particular attention to those who guaranteed its vital interests; for example, Rhodes would always come down in favour of Byzantium because it was the guardian of the Bosphorus.

Does it not seem amusing to think that a city, Rhodes, which today has around 70,000 inhabitants was the protector of one which today has almost fifteen million: modern-day Istanbul? This is what is fascinating about history!

Keeping open the straits of the Bosphorus and the Dardanelles. I have just noted the role of guardian angel which Rhodes always adopted in respect of Byzantium, but it also did so with respect to Sinope and other centres on the Black Sea.
It was an obvious political choice; the place in question was the point of access to the second vital market for sourcing.

The enemies of Rhodes

Well then, did this champion of peace and compromise not have enemies and did it not fight against anybody?

Obviously, it did.

There were four principal adversaries for Rhodes, but always for rational motives and not from ideological choice: Macedonia, Pergamon, Crete and Lycia.

Macedonia emerged from the 'Wars of the Diadochi' as the militarily strongest and most aggressive state among those of Alexander's former generals.

Rhodes tried to keep its distance and placate it as far as possible, but it was Macedonia that several times set out to disturb the peace.

If we add that Macedonia was constantly the enemy of the friend Egypt and that it was located geographically by the straits accessing the Black Sea, then the preconditions for an enmity based on strategic reasons are complete.

Nevertheless, in its dealings with such a preponderant power, Rhodes always sought an accommodation. When this was not possible, it led to the Great Siege of 305 and, a century later, to the appeal Rhodes made to Rome, specifically for help against the Macedonians.

Pergamon, however, was not so strong. Nevertheless, geo-politically, it had designs on the straits of access to the Black Sea.

The history of relations between the two states appears marked by a succession of skirmishes and antipathies than open conflicts. For example, Pergamon was the only place not to help Rhodes after the earthquake of 228. However, when Rome established itself in the eastern Mediterranean, both Rome and Pergamon were its closest allies and, willy-nilly, Rome forced them to pretend to get along.

On the other hand, no compromise was possible with Crete. This island was the biggest den of pirates at the time, and who more than a pirate damages a merchant marine? The history of the relations between the republic of Rhodes and Crete is a story of constant conflict. Fortunately, Crete was seldom a coherent whole; accordingly, it was almost always divided into rival city alliances. With great skill Rhodian diplomacy managed to facilitate the fratricidal struggles among the various Cretan cities, enjoying the advantages of proxy wars and limiting as far as possible its own direct interventions.

To explain the constant hostility with Lycia, it is necessary now to talk about Peraea, somewhere we have already come across in the preceding chapter.

Control over Peraea and the southern Dodecanese

Peraea was a strip of land, the Loryma Peninsula and a half-moon shaped piece of land surrounding it on the coast of Anatolia located opposite the island of Rhodes.

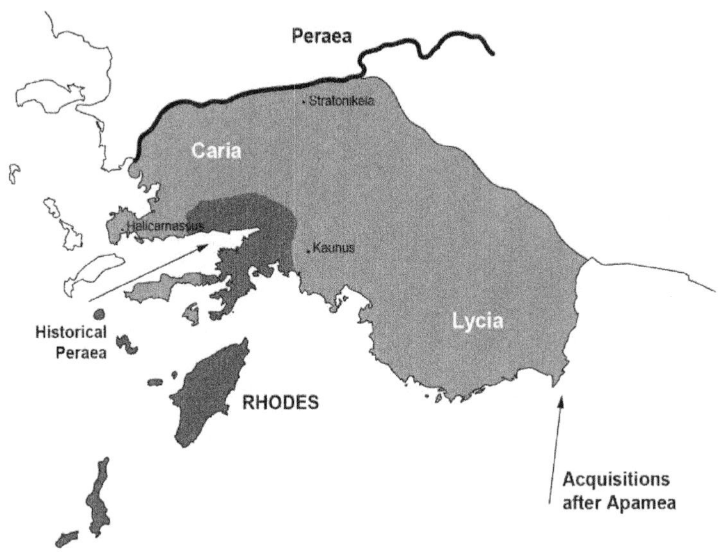

Its strategic importance is clear: control of both sides of the strait; availability of a landing place on the continent; supply of wood. In addition, Rhodes was very attracted by the fertile plane to the east of today's Marmaris. Let us not forget that Rhodes itself is a mountain rising out of the sea.

In Peraea the residents had full Rhodian citizenship and were also divided among themselves among the three 'mother cities': no more or no less than those who lived on the island. The centres were small agglomerations of houses, but all had an acropolis, a small theatre and some kind of defensive structure, a wall or a 'shelter', that is to say a raised fortification into which the inhabitants could retreat in times of danger.

Of these centres the most prominent, moving from east to west, were: Phiskos, today's Marmaris, which belonged to Lindos; Tloi, today's Serçe Limani on the Loryma Peninsula, a dependency of Kameiros; Loryma itself and further to the north Bybassos, located at the north-western tip of the Loryma Peninsula. We do not know to which of the Rhodian cities the last two town were related.

Rhodes always sought to expand into the surrounding areas from this 'historical' Peraea, above all because at that time supremacy meant wealth; for example, the archives have revealed to us the sum of the tributes imposed on the two main subjugated cities, Kaunus and Stratonicea: by no means chicken feed. Moreover, Rhodes always wished to expand to protect the Peraea itself better, in accordance with what students of military behaviour call 'strategic depth'. We shall see how, in the Hellenistic era, Peraea will also be fortified with the great fort of Loryma.

To understand the geographical directions for possible expansions of Peraea it is sufficient to look at a relief map. The mountains behind provided an adequate barrier against aggressive ambitions against, either against or from the neighbours.

Expansion was only possible along the coast, both northwards towards Caria and to the east towards today's Antalya, what at that time was Lycia. Whereas the people of Caria always had cordial relations with Rhodes (let us not forget that their principal city was Halicarnassus, a historical ally of Rhodes), the relationship with Lycia was one of constant tensions and rebellions. Nevertheless, these amounted to minor events within the grand narrative of the history of Rhodes.

Speaking of the rather modest aspirations of territorial expansion on the part of Rhodes, when all is considered, I will add that the island also dominated all the surrounding archipelago of the southern Dodecanese: Karpathos, Xalki and Symi from the beginning, and Kastellorizo, Kasos, Nisyros and Thilos from the fourth century B.C..

The walls of Rhodes and their history over the centuries

Having spoken of war, it is natural to describe the military system.

To put it in a nutshell: Rhodes had a very strong navy, whilst the army was always marginal. Its only role was to patrol the interior with the real defence on land being focused on the city walls.

Here we come to one of my pet subjects: the walls of the city of Rhodes. I am allowing myself a digression which is partly outside the focus of this book. Anyone not interested can simply jump to the next chapter.

Every time that I am on Rhodes I pass through the imposing medieval city walls, sometimes even several times a day, and each time is an emotional experience.

Hellenistic and Medieval Walls of Rhodes

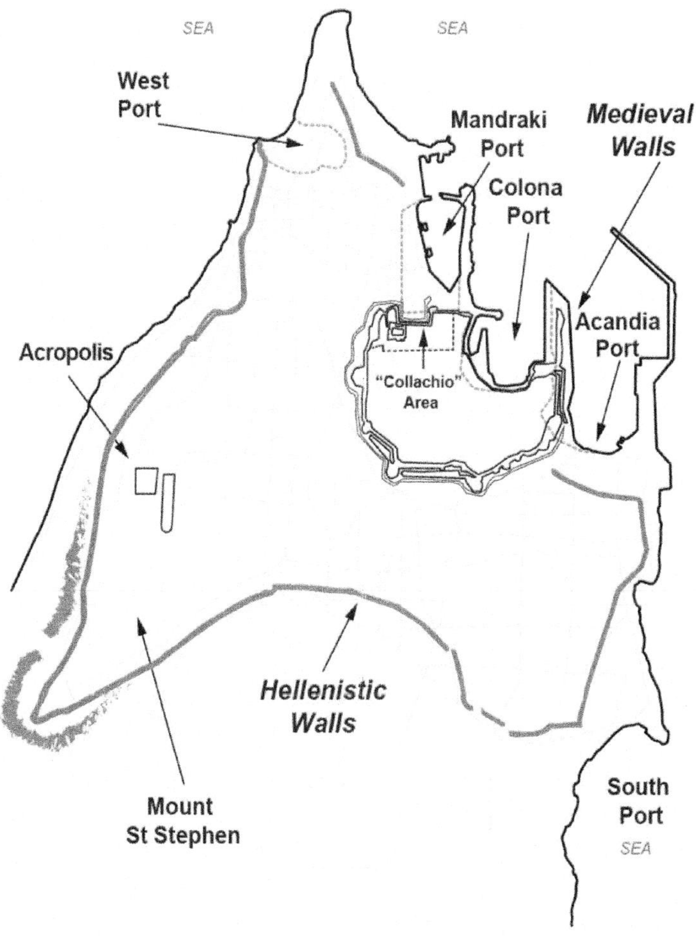

The architectural and historical leap which takes place in the space of a few metres is incredible, especially for those not entering from the north, where there are more monuments but where everything is disfigured by mass tourism, but from the working-class districts through the gates of St Athanasius (sometimes called of *San Francesco*) or of St John (sometimes called of *Koskinou* or the 'red gate'). Here many people live in basic dwellings at street level, similar to those known in Naples as 'bassi', and especially in summer there is a sense of real life, with the women sitting on the house steps, holding court, and with families dining around a table placed directly in front of the door.

We are talking perhaps of the most complete and best-preserved medieval walls in the world: a monument, which can boast more than twenty-four centuries of history.

I have already spoken of the walls planned by Hippodamus and of how they were constantly reinforced throughout the fourth century. We shall see in the next chapter how this defensive system was strong enough to save the city from the siege of the Macedonian army and how, shortly afterwards, the city was extended because of the growth of the economy and the population, and a new enclosing wall was built. Finally, we shall see that these Hellenistic walls were not able, in the years of decline, to stop the ultimately modest army of Cassius, one of Caesar's assassins, in 42 B.C..

It is with these events that the period which I have chosen to narrate will end, and accordingly the book as well. However, this is not the end of the great story of the walls of Rhodes. This brief overview of the events around the walls of Rhodes is also an opportunity to sketch the later history of the island: from the time of the Roman Empire until our times.

During the long years of the *pax romana* the walls were not relevant; I therefore imagine that they were not subject to major investment. They became essential again as an instrument of defence during the progressive decline of the Byzantine Empire, let us say from the end of the sixth century A.D.. In the absence of imperial protection Rhodes had to rely on itself, and thus as a first step reinforced the walls. However, this was not a negligible expense in a situation of economic and demographic impoverishment. Rhodes tried to do its best: the powerful hid themselves away on the inside of a final wall-like, although not very strong, enclosure in the north western part of the city (still identifiable): the Collachio. In addition, the city shrank from the south side to end up well inside the old Hellenistic walls. Whoever walks down today's Pythagoras Street in the old city, for example, runs into what remains of the fortifications built, somehow or other, with demolished materials from earlier buildings.

These were obviously defensive works of limited value, which did not prevent the capture of the city by whoever turned up with some strength. And the list of those who took and sacked Rhodes in these dark years is unfortunately very long. The Goths set the ball rolling in 263 A.D., but fortunately this was still an isolated incident. In 620 it was the turn of the Persians, and shortly afterwards, in 653, the Saracen pirates arrived. Next in line were the Turks of the Seljuq Dynasty in 807, followed in 1123 by the Venetians. In 1191 Richard the Lionheart, passing through Rhodes for the Crusades, imposed levies; in 1248 the Genoese had the idea of plundering the Rhodians.

The situation changed from 1309 when Rhodes, without a blow being struck, fell into the hands of the knights. The Knights of St John or Hospitaliers, subsequently Knights 'of Rhodes' and thereafter 'of Malta' were the last military corps organized with the mission to defend the territory that remained in the hands of the crusaders in the Holy Land. When, however, they were expelled from their final stronghold in Palestine, St John of Acre, they began to wander around the Mediterranean in search of headquarters. Their peregrinations came to an end when in fact they occupied Rhodes, at that time nominally part of the Byzantine Empire. I do not wish to expand on this glorious period about which, moreover, very much has been written. What is important here is the efforts of the knights to reconstruct the walls. Their work is what we still see today.

They used the best techniques of the time, devoted major financial resources and engaged the most renowned military architects. The proof of this is that the walls stoutly resisted the siege of 1444 by the Sultan of Egypt who withdrew licking his wounds. The same thing happened in 1480 with the siege of Mehmed II, who was certainly not wet behind the ears; in 1453 he had stormed Constantinople, the last Roman capital, putting an end to the Byzantine Empire.

Over the next forty years the works to reinforce the walls proceeded without interruption and again Rhodes availed itself of the best available technology of the time. Particularly worthy of mention are the fabled

Grand Master D'Amboise and, in the following years, the military engineer Gabriele Tadino di Martinengo.

Time passed until 1522, when the walls held out against Suleiman the Magnificent. Tadino was still present during the siege to reinforce the walls day by day. When at the end of the same year the Turks took control of Rhodes, it was not a case of conquest, but an agreed surrender. The Turkish sultan decided to concede safe passage to the defenders who left because they had been abandoned by the Pope and the Catholic west (how far gone was the spirit of the crusades!).

Perhaps the outcome would have been the same, but the fact is that in 1522 the walls of Rhodes resisted for eight months the siege of an army almost a hundred times larger than the number of defenders and were not overcome! This was the last time that they served to defend the city against a siege.

Just as an aside, Suleiman had very good reason to regret letting the defenders of Rhodes go. He was confronted by Tadino, acting as commander of the artillery, during his abortive attempt to conquer Vienna in 1532, whilst in 1565 the Knights repulsed him in Malta where they had set themselves up in the meantime.

In the following 390 years Rhodes lived under the *pax ottomana,* with no enemy in sight. Nevertheless, the walls still had their uses. For the Turks, the conquest of Rhodes was important to eradicate an advanced Christian outpost inside their own territory, but there was no strategic interest in running the city as such.

In the city of Rhodes, the Turks only had a military garrison of modest size, complemented by some civilians, mainly artisans. They followed the same pattern on Kos. In the remaining parts of the two islands, as well as in the other Dodecanese islands, there was almost no Turkish presence; they frequently restricted themselves to an annual symbolic display of authority by gathering a tribute.

Even in Rhodes City, where in fact the Turkish community was not insignificant numerically, the Turks perceived themselves as a minority. They used the walls to enclose themselves inside from dusk to dawn in a kind of self-imposed ghetto. Alongside them were their most faithful allies, the Sephardic Jews, welcomed in Rhodes by none other than the Turks, some years after their expulsion from Spain at the end of the fifteenth century.

The Greeks were expelled from the old city. And so, they went where there was space: just outside of the walled city, to the south. There the 'Marassia' grew up, groups of tightly-packed dwellings around their own church, an area which still today surrounds the old town like a crown. It is also to be noted that from the sixteenth century onwards some churches were built in the Marassia, one of which is the Mitropoli (seat of the Patriarch), these being among the most beautiful orthodox churches of the city.

In view of the weakness of the Turkish garrison, it comes as no surprise that on 16 May 1912 the Italian armed forces, the last of the invaders, were able to enter the old city almost without firing a shot. This is when the last phase of the epic story of the walls of Rhodes began. They became a monument. Thanks to the Italian government and archaeologists, the walls (and with them the whole of the old city) were renovated and restored.

New entrances were opened up to allow the walled city to breathe and, with a solemn ceremony, after exactly four hundred years the gate of St Athanasius was reopened. This gate had been closed by the Turks because Suleiman the Magnificent had entered the conquered city of the crusaders through it, on foot, and no normal mortal could be allowed to tread in the footsteps of the great sultan!

Chapter Four

The days of glory: from 323 to 188 B.C.

Independence – The Diadochi Wars – The 'Great Siege' – The Hellenistic Walls – The Acropolis –The Colossus – New York, Liberty Island: the Statue of Liberty – The fort of Loryma –The political events of the Third Century – The earthquake of 228 B.C. – Philip V and the First Macedonian War –The second Macedonian War – The Syrian War and the Peace of Apamea – Rome has arrived

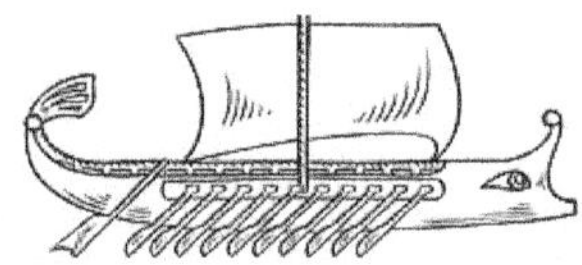

Independence

Let us resume the chronological narrative where we left it two chapters ago.

In the summer of 323, in distant Babylon, Alexander the Great died and the people of Rhodes profited by expelling the Macedonian garrisons and finally becoming independent. They did not have further ambitions and thus they wisely steered clear of the misguided pan-Hellenic revolt led by Athens.

The Diadochi Wars

The Diadochi, the warlords of Alexander, immediately began to fight against one another over the division of the legacy of the Emperor and, after various twists and turns, there emerged three main states, which, on the basis of the balance of power among them, dominated the eastern Mediterranean until the arrival of the Romans, around 130 years later.

There was Macedonia where Antigonus Monophtalmus (one-eye) reigned. Of the three states it was the most cohesive and militarily the strongest. Then there was Egypt, in the hands of Ptolemy, the richest because of its agricultural resources. The third, where Seleucus Nicator held sway, was a vast territory extending from the Mediterranean coast of Syria to Iran, but with too many frontiers to defend and thus always weakened by sudden attacks from various directions.

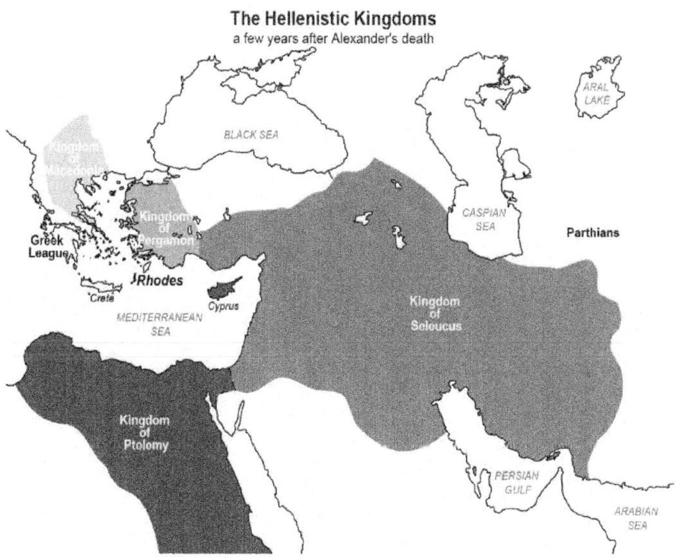

In the areas interspersed among the three big states there were independent, or perhaps, given the size of their neighbours, it would be more correct to say semi-independent, smaller entities located in western Anatolia, in the Aegean and Greece itself. This was the theatre of action for Rhodes which was located in this area and was probably the most important of these entities, and certainly the richest.

For eight years Alexander's generals were too busy fighting one another. Rhodes was left in peace and the republic profited to pursue its business interests and to reinforce the walls, acting in a coherent manner in accordance with the political strategy described in the previous chapter. The one exception: in 321 there appeared on the scene a minor warlord, a certain Attalos, who was roundly defeated.

However, in 315, certainly in spite of itself, Rhodes was called on to make a choice. Antigonus, who was at war with Ptolemy, demanded an alliance. Rhodes deployed all its diplomatic skills and, in fact, got away with building some warships for Antigonus (who obviously had to pay for them!) and lending lukewarm support with some contingents from Rhodes supporting the Macedonians during the siege of Tyre, whilst at the same time managing to cultivate its friendship with Ptolemy without making him fly off the handle. Brilliant!

In 312 Antigonus tried again to involve them, but Rhodes only gave him a contingent of ten warships. As this was practically nothing, Rhodes had managed once more to stay neutral without annoying either of the two warring parties.

Once more in 306 an analogous situation presented itself. Antigonus was attacking Egypt again and again he asked Rhodes for support. The situation was now more critical than on the two previous occasions, because the relative strength of

Macedonia compared with Egypt had further increased. Thus, the space for diplomatic manoeuvres by Rhodes was more limited, but the island would have been inclined to any compromise to avoid worse damage.

Unfortunately, there were two demands to which Rhodes could not give in: declare war on Ptolemy, king of the country, commercial relations with which provided the basis for its wealth and strength and, above all, accept Macedonian ships inside its own port. That would have amounted *de facto* to being annexed to Macedonia, the end of independence. For the only time in the history of the maritime republic, Rhodes decided to go for broke and rejected the request of Antigonus.

The 'Great Siege'

The reaction was not long in coming. In the summer of 305 B.C. Antigonus sent his son Demetrius to attack Rhodes, whose inhabitants had taken refuge inside the walls. The 'Great Siege' had begun.

Thanks to the classical authors, we know much about it and it is a fascinating story full of dramatic events. It could be the plot of an action movie, if one also takes into account the surprising number of analogies with the sieges of almost two thousand years later: those of Mehmed II in 1480 and Suleiman the Magnificent in 1522. It is almost incredible to see how little siege tactics had changed over the centuries.

Demetrius, first of all, occupied Peraea and concentrated his forces at Loryma, on the shore of

Anatolia opposite Rhodes (and it was here that the Turkish sultans as well concentrated their men in 1480 and 1522).

Demetrius had an imposing army at his disposal: 40,000 infantrymen and an unknown number of knights, 200 warships and 170 transport ships. Furthermore, many thousands of pirates and 'merchants' had joined him with their accompanying ships (could the number be estimated at a thousand?), along with some eager irregular forces all intent on participating in the expected sacking of the city.

The large armada paraded slowly in front of the walls of Rhodes in order to intimidate the defenders and went off to disembark south of the city. It is not known if they went to the west to the Bay of Trianda, as Mehmed II did in 1480, or to the east to Kalithea Bay, as Suleiman did in 1522. What is certain is that, like both his illustrious successors, Demetrius set up his headquarters on Mount Filerimos.

The balance of forces in terms of men was greatly unequal: more than ten to one. Against Demetrius, Rhodes had only 6,000 city hoplites and a number of lightly armed soldiers. A thousand foreigners residing in the city joined them, the others were expelled. It is significant to note that only one in six of the foreigners took up arms in defence, indicating the lack of attachment to the fate of the city by those who were there only for mercantile interests: a "multicultural" society does not only bring advantages.

However, this kind of disparity was always to be a characteristic of the sieges of Rhodes; historical sources, possibly exaggerating a bit, speak of 100,000 assailants against 3,500 defenders in 1480 and even 200,000 against 6,000 in 1522. The defence of the city, as we have already seen, was entrusted to the walls!

The bulk of the Macedonian troops were encamped to the south of the city, but others were also positioned to the north between the walled city and the extreme point of the island, where today there is the district of Neochori.

Demetrius, like the Turkish sultans later, launched his first attacks from the side of the sea where the city fortifications appeared weakest. On some of their ships, the Macedonians constructed real purpose-built towers to allow their archers to rise above the level of the walls. They persisted with this tactic for almost a week but did not manage to overcome the defences. They reorganised for a week and then tried again. But things went worse this time. The Rhodian fleet made a sortie with specially chosen crews led by the navarch Execestus and destroyed two important siege towers. The two sides were far from being evenly matched when it came to a clash between the technical capabilities of the crews of the two fleets!

Demetrius though was an obstinate fellow and made a further attempt to attack from the sea. He began to construct within the harbour a further siege tower, three times more imposing than the previous ones, but, with the aid of a day of bad weather (a heartfelt 'thank you' to Apollo Helios), the Rhodians undertook a further sortie, destroyed the construction and even managed to capture 400 enemies. In the meantime, the morale of the defenders had been reinforced; the allied Cretan city of Knossos had sent them 150 fighters and Egypt major supplies of food and 500 mercenaries.

We have now reached the start of the year 304. Demetrius decided to change tactics and attack from the land. He dug tunnels in order to light fires under the walls; the Rhodians defended themselves with tunnels which today we would call 'countermining'. There's no need to say that the same thing happened during the sieges of Mehmed and Suleiman!

However, Demetrius sought primarily to exploit the military technology of the age to the maximum. He entrusted to the architect Epimachus of Athens the construction of a Helepolis. This was a siege tower almost fifty metres high. To make this clear: it is the equivalent of an eighteen-storey block nowadays! The Helepolis was planned with nine terraces to support artillery machines. It was the most imposing siege machine ever built and it earned Demetrius, among other things, the everlasting sobriquet of 'Poliorcetes': the besieger. 30,000 men were at work on the towers and the tunnels.

In the meantime, the Rhodians, too, were preparing, demolishing houses to recover building materials to erect a second circle of wall at the points where the attack was expected.

Rhodes did not limit itself to defence but counterattacked. In fact, it put to sea as many as three fleets each with its own commander. Damophilus went to Karpathos, Menedemus to the coast of Lycia, Amyntas patrolled around the island of Rhodes itself. All the three fleets attacked Demetrius' ships and captured supplies and military reinforcements, sowing confusion in the enemy camp. The naval supremacy of the Rhodians was absolute. It also meant that the city could not be cut off from the sea.

In the meantime, the Rhodians confirmed, if we ever had any doubts about it, that they still had a head for business. Whilst they were fighting for survival, one eye was directed to the post-siege conditions of peace, conscious that it could only be based on compromise. Accordingly, in order not to cause irritation, Rhodes decided not to demolish the statues of Antigonus and Demetrius, erected in the previous years, when it maintained the pretence of being friends.

Finally, the hour for the attack arrived. Everything was ready on the Macedonian side. A vast area around Helepolis was totally deforested, eight canopies surrounded it to protect the engineers, two reinforced sheds with battering rams inside accompanied them to the walls. To disperse the defence forces, the assailants launched various attacks all along the rim of the city both from the sea and the land.

But a new development made Demetrius suspend the attack. Ambassadors from Knidos had arrived to try to broker an agreement. But there being no give on either side, the attack restarted. The attackers literally battered down a section of wall. The Rhodians took refuge inside the second enclosure. In this desperate situation, a little moral comfort was provided by the arrival of food supplies sent by all the Hellenistic sovereigns who were enemies of Antigonus: Ptolemy as usual, but also sovereigns of minor states such as Cassander and Lysimachus.

Nevertheless, it was a critical moment but 'when the going gets tough, the tough get going'. There were no strategic alternatives; the Rhodians had their backs to the wall with no escape any more. All they could do was try a counterattack. They did this on a grand scale, waited for a moonless night and threw all the artillery they had into the battle. In the space of a few hours, 800 fireballs and 1500 projectiles launched from catapults rained down on the amazed Demetrius. The counterattack succeeded. The Helepolis was set ablaze, if not destroyed, but Demetrius now needed time to repair it, time which the Rhodians used in their turn to repair the walls. Simultaneously they put another fleet to sea and set off to defeat Timocles, a pirate allied to Demetrius.

While preparing the next attack, Demetrius was interrupted by around fifty peace missions from the same number of Greek cities. Meanwhile Rhodes was reinforced by more supplies of food and, above all, by 1,500 fighters from Egypt.

As in the key moment of an action movie, the two sides were ready for the second largescale attack: only this time Demetrius could not launch it because of orders from above!

The *deus ex machina* who saved Rhodes was Seleucus, the ruler of the mighty Syria. The third of the major Hellenistic monarchs was increasingly worried at the military superiority of Antigonus over Ptolemy. He knew that a collapse of the latter would have left his state in a vise between Macedonia and Egypt, both subject to Antigonus Monophthalmus. This was a nightmare scenario; he decided therefore to intervene militarily on the side of Ptolemy. At this point it was the turn of Antigonus to be in difficulties and to need all his troops. He recalled his son from the siege of Rhodes.

Demetrius and Rhodes rapidly reached an agreement, which saved the face of the former but was in fact a victory of the latter. Rhodes accepted all the conditions which Macedonia had previously demanded of it and formally became one of its allies.

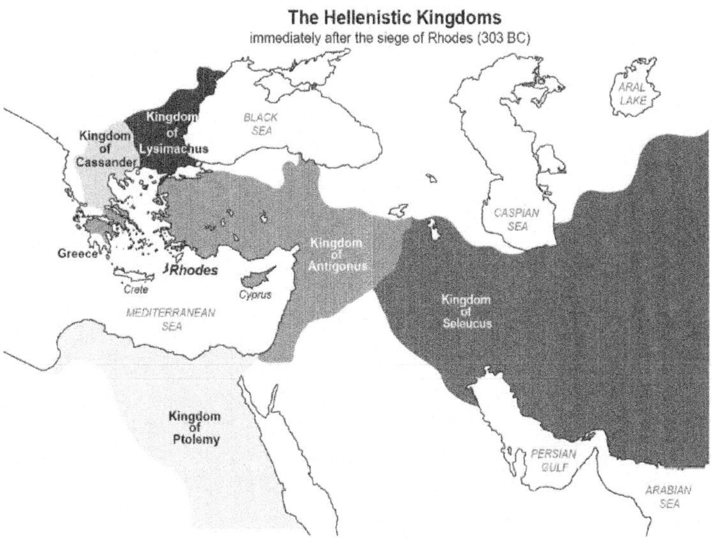

Only two of the previous demands were not accepted, conveniently those which had unleashed the war! No Macedonian ship or contingent was to enter the walls, whilst the island would indeed be the ally of Macedonia, but not in the case of a conflict with Egypt. Excuse me, but in that case what are we talking about? Furthermore, to cover the war damage, Demetrius left behind his celebrated war machines by way of reparations. The profits from their sale would form the financial nucleus for the construction of the famous Colossus.

It was the apotheosis. Rhodes was already rich, already had a potent fleet, but in 305 it had survived its baptism of fire: against the strongest military power of the time. And it had come out victorious!

Rhodes celebrated itself. It built a new surrounding wall, greatly expanding the city of the Dorieus era. It erected a monumental area on the Acropolis and, something which is much better known, between 304 and 293 it also built the Colossus. Let us tell the story of these developments.

The Hellenistic Walls

The previous walls, built from 408 B.C. onwards and always progressively strengthened and kept maintained, had withstood magnificently all assaults, as we have seen from the siege of Poliorcetes. However, Rhodes was overwhelmed by its own commercial success; the influx of an even greater number of persons made necessary an extension of the city and thus the construction of a new enclosing wall. So, there were built what we know as the 'Hellenistic Walls'.

Let us begin with their placement: the city could obviously only expand where there was space. To the east it was already by the sea, to the west all the possible land, which did not amount to much, was taken over: the slope descending beyond Mount St

Stephen down to the sea. The city also expanded to the north. There was not much room and it tended to be marshy, but it was strategic. Demetrius had positioned a part of his army to the north of the city outside the walls, thus closing it off from two sides and this was a mistake Rhodes did not wish to repeat. Moreover, moving the system of defence to the north also meant better military protection for the two ports: Mandraki and the northern port. Significant archaeological discoveries of protective works are visible to those who venture near today's lyric theatre. For reasons of topographical necessity, however, the main direction for expansion was, then as now, to the south.

Examining the plan of the Hellenistic extension, we note that it had a curious form, like an arrowhead. The tip is to the north, at the sides the diverging walls follow the two coastlines, whilst to the south it has a curious form like a swallow's tail in order to follow the hollows of the terrain.

To describe the Hellenistic walls of Rhodes is, however, difficult and from certain points of view inappropriate. Above all, there was not a single surrounding wall; inside the external wall there were secondary walls and various fortifications, partially built from scratch and partially reusing defensive structures of the pre-existing city. Secondly, there was not a unified project, pre-defined down to the last detail, but 'a work in progress' lasting more than seventy years. What has been reconstructed today as the 'definitive line' is the wall of 227 B.C., after the great earthquake of the preceding year.

Hellenistic City

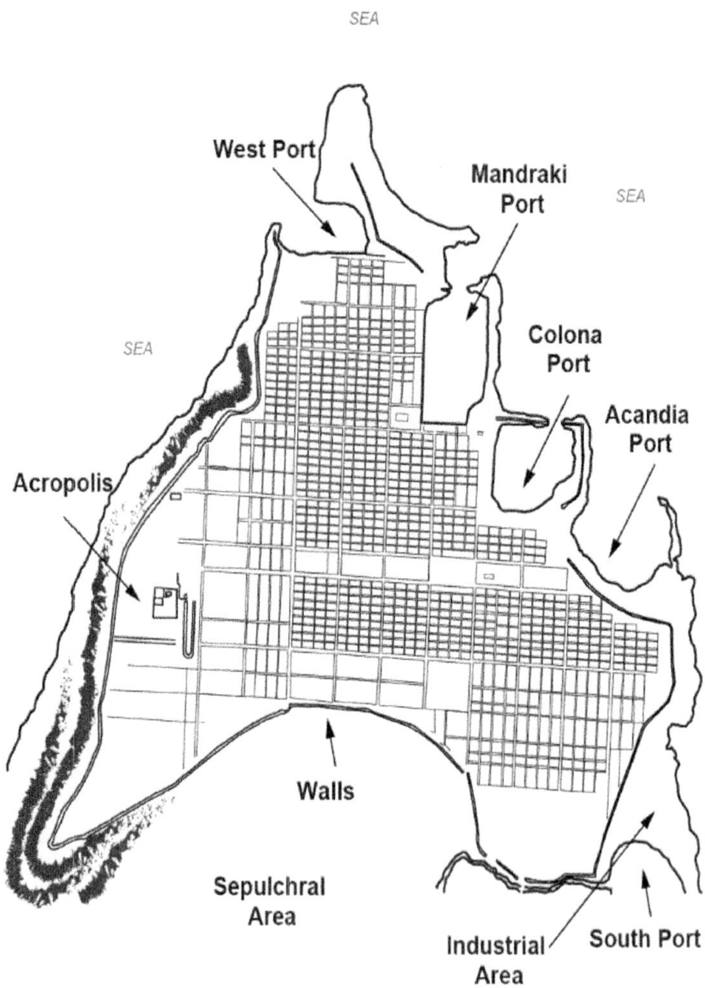

The Hellenistic walls were destroyed in large measure over the centuries: by force of arms and earthquakes, but above all by a systematic work of dismantlement on the part of the inhabitants of Rhodes themselves, who for almost twenty centuries used them as a quarry to construct their own buildings. When the Italian occupiers, in the first half of the twentieth century, put a stop to this practice, it was too late; the damage was done. If we add that there was a lot of building on a large part of the surrounding wall in successive centuries and that today a significant part of the Hellenistic walls lies underneath buildings, the extent of the difficulties that archaeologists have had to face in studying them becomes clear.

I have stressed how the Hellenistic walls became for centuries the quarry for subsequent building activity. But what was the quarry for the stones used to build them? Probably the usual cliffs of the Bay of Kalithea, but in large measure it was Mount St Stephen. To build the Hellenistic Acropolis, enormous terraces were cut out, suitable to support the monuments; the stone removed was thus used to build the walls.

The Acropolis

This information takes us to the story of the second great work of the beginning of the third century: the construction of the Acropolis. I have already recounted that the principal temple of the city of Hippodamus, the one dedicated to the protective god, Apollo Helios, was positioned in front of where the palace of the Grand Master is located. On the site stands now a school from the Turkish era.

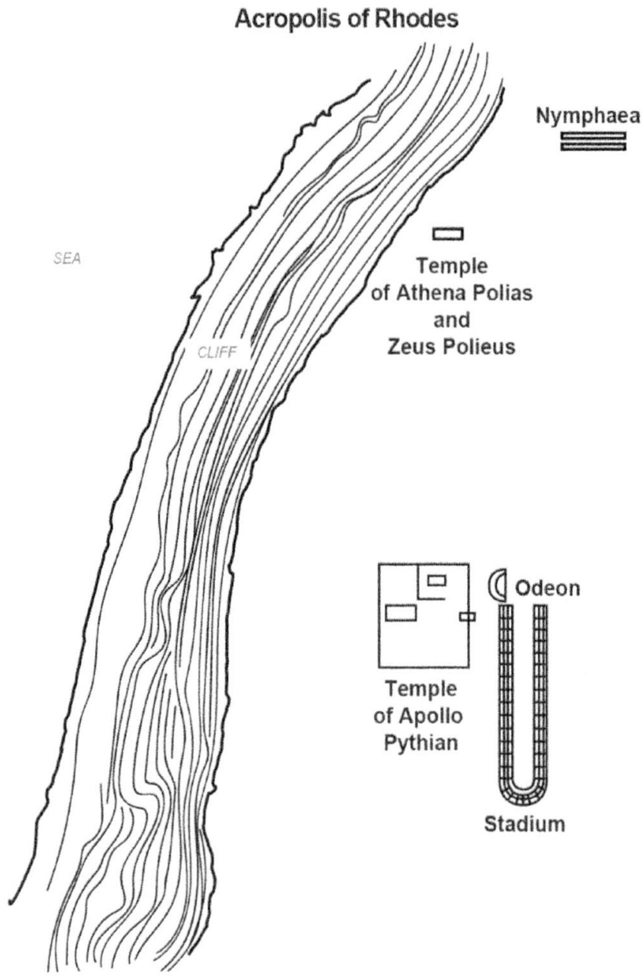
Acropolis of Rhodes
Nymphaea
SEA
CLIFF
Temple
of Athena Polias
and
Zeus Polieus
Odeon
Temple
of Apollo
Pythian
Stadium

However, right from the birth of the city of Rhodes sacred buildings were constructed, including some on Mount St Stephen, the high ground which, with its height of 88 metres, dominates and delimits the city itself to the west. The largest of the temples located there dates back to this epoch: it is the one dedicated to the god Apollo, this time not 'Helios', god of the sun, but in his role of 'Pythian', that is to say oracle. Architecturally, it was a typical temple in the Doric style from the late classical era and its dimensions provided for six columns at the front and eleven at the sides. We do not know its exact dimensions, but it was imposing. To give an idea: the temple of Concordia at Agrigento, this, too, with six and eleven columns, has an area of 800 sq. metres, just less than half of that of the most important of classical Greek temples, the Parthenon in Athens, which happens to have been completed at the same time.

However, it was only after the great siege that the Acropolis became the important sacred area, which we know or, more precisely, pretend to know.

The Acropolis extended over an area principally consisting of the great terraces cut out as described above and included numerous buildings.

At the northern limits of the area, there was the temple dedicated to Athena Polias and Zeus Polieus, chosen to be the protectors of the city. And there can be no doubt about this; Polias and Polieus, feminine and masculine respectively, mean 'citizen'. Among other things, this temple was used to house the most important documents and international treaties: a kind of state archive. It was a typical Rhodian temple of the late classical and Hellenistic era: of small dimensions, with a certain mixture of the three styles, Doric-Ionic-Corinthian, more elegant on the inside, where it was adorned with stucco and brightly colored frescoes, than on the outside, where the rusticated sandstone gave an intentional sense of 'unfinished'.

Further to the south the previous temple of Apollo Pythian, already referred to, was located. However, the best-preserved monument is the stadium of about 210 metres in length and with the very characteristic 'U' shape. Other significant monuments include four Nymphaea, underground grottoes intended for religious purposes, and an Odeon, a theatre with only 800 places and therefore very modest for the city of Rhodes, probably intended for concerts of cultured music.

Centuries of earthquakes, wars and abandonment have almost destroyed the Acropolis. Only a major project, begun by Italian archaeologists in the 20s and 30s of the last century, has restarted scientific study of the site. The love of these experts for the antiquities of the island is palpable if one reads the back numbers of *Clara Rhodos*, the review of the Historical and Archaeological Institute of Rhodes, published precisely in those years, between 1928 and 1941.

However, apart from the stadium, anyone who sets foot on the Acropolis today, I mean a lay person like me, can take in little of the ancient splendour; the great temple of Apollo consists today of just three pillars rebuilt by the Italian archaeologists. At the cost of repeating, but it is my view that the best way to get an idea of what the Acropolis of Rhodes was like is to go to Agrigento where the Temple of Concordia, built by cousins of the ancient Rhodians is the best and more lifelike model.

To complete the topic, it should also be said that temples and sporting buildings were not restricted to the Acropolis but were spread throughout the city. To give an example the great Ptolemaic Gymnasium, of which today we only know its vast dimensions, was located just south of today's Diagoras Stadium. Like the cemeteries and the factories, the sporting facilities on Rhodes also tend to stick to the same areas over the centuries!

The Colossus

Of all the great self-celebrations of Rhodes after the siege of 305 B.C., I have left until last the third leg: 'the icing on the cake', the Colossus, one of the seven wonders of the ancient world.

Writing a few words about the Colossus is a reputational risk for anybody, even an amateur historian like me. Although much has been written, too much of it is controversial; therefore, here I will only record what to me seems most sensible.

It was a gigantesque statue dedicated to Apollo Helios and was designed and executed by Chares of Lindos, thus a son of the island. He had been the pupil of one of the most important sculptors of classical Greece, Lysippos to whose brief stay on the island I have already referred. We also know the name of the high priest, Diosippos, he too from Lindos, who added the final signature to authorise the construction.

The Colossus was 32 metres high. Furthermore, it is assumed that it was placed on a circular pedestal higher than fifteen metres. Accordingly, all in all, it was as high as today's buildings of about sixteen storeys. Thus, it goes without saying that it was 'visible from the sea and from the Asian continent', as an anonymous author of the time described it. It should be borne in mind that the local regulations of Rhodes, as a precaution against earthquakes, allowed houses up to two storeys and that probably only a few odd public buildings were slightly higher.

It represented Apollo Helios, curly haired and crowned by sun's rays, as we know from Rhodian coins of that era; he had a quiver on his shoulders and held the torch of liberty in his hands. The latter was called Phosphoros; it was meant to represent the planet Venus when dawn is about to break. It is a matter of dispute whether the quiver as well was a sculpture covered with bronze wires to reflect the sun's rays or a fire kept permanently alight meant to act as a lighthouse for all the ports of Rhodes. The legs of the stature were apart. Being a sun god, he turned his shoulders to the east to look westwards, as we have already noted in relation to the quadriga donated to Delphi.

An anonymous dedication of the time salutes him as follows:

To you, O Helios, the people of Dorian Rhodes set up this bronze statue reaching to Olympus when they had pacified the waves of war and crowned their city with the spoils taken from the enemy. Not only over the seas but also on land did they kindle the lovely torch of freedom, because for the descendants of the line of Hercules belongs dominion over sea and land.

There is no denying that this is a programmatic manifesto! What strikes me is that, despite the changing and opportunistic political alliances, still in the third century, the Dorian origin of the islanders was still fully present and strongly reaffirmed, twice within a few lines: 'Dorian Rhodes' and 'the line of Hercules' are ways of stating this.

The Colossus was made of hollow bronze held up by an internal structure of iron bars and stone. It definitely had a triangular base because it would not have been stable on two legs and possibly would have even collapsed under its own weight. We can only hypothesise about the third support: a sword? The edge of a cloak? The iconography of the Romantic period in the 1800s represents it held up only by two legs, which is certainly incorrect for obvious reasons of structural engineering.

Unfortunately, it did not last long. As early as 228 a violent earthquake caused it to topple, breaking it at knee height. The rational Rhodians, I imagine after a complex exercise of double-entry bookkeeping in the manner of good businessmen, decided that the cost of reconstruction was excessive in relation to the benefits in terms of image. Obviously, it was not their decision; they had it pronounced by an oracle...

We now come to the most debated question: where was it placed?

It was certainly not on Mandraki port, as the wishful thinking of the nineteenth-century Romantics had it:

where could the tripod of the statue have been put? How could it have been turned to the west if the mouth of the port opened to the north? Once collapsed, it would have closed the port; however, this was always active although the ruins of the Colossus remained *in situ* for almost 900 years. Moreover, the statue was indeed broken, but still an object of admiration, so much so that Pliny the Elder, who saw it in the first century B.C., was still able to describe its imposing form. It is difficult to imagine it so easily accessible if it had been at the bottom of the sea. And then, just having had their fingers burned from the experience of a siege, would the ancient Rhodians have placed such an expensive object outside the city wall, an easy prey to any future aggressor?

There are two plausible alternatives. We have seen that in those very years the sacred area of the Acropolis was constructed and the Colossus could have been built there. The alternative would be inside the city of Hippodamus, in the old holy area, in front of the current Grand Master's Palace. It was there that the oldest temple of Apollo Helios had been built; according to this school of thought, the old temple would have been replaced by the colossal statue of the same god during the reconstruction of the city after the siege.

For me, the second hypothesis is more convincing. First of all, there are no further mentions of the oldest temple of Apollo in the city, which would be very strange if it had remained standing. Secondly, the area in question is right in the centre and, before the building of the St John's Cathedral by the knights in the fourteen century, it is improbable that there would have been no building of importance. What would be more rational than to think that this site played host first to the Colossus, and thereafter to its ruins, for almost 1000 years?

As to the Acropolis, it has been comprehensively excavated and nothing resembling remnants of the ancient statue have emerged. By contrast, in the area of St John's Cathedral still today there is a building, a school from the Turkish era, that I have already mentioned. Accordingly, it is not only difficult to excavate, but above all whatever was there previously was certainly removed and tampered with.

I will just add that the Colossus was built between 304 and 293 B.C., years in which the Acropolis was being excavated for cutting the terraces; was it not better to build the great statue in an already prepared area?

Finally, there is a linguistic dimension. When in the high medieval period, therefore a time of exclusively Greek culture, the Byzantines enclosed this area with new walls, they called it 'Collachio'. This is a word which does not appear to mean anything in the Greek language, whilst in terms of sound it appears to share a common root with 'Colossus'. What is more, the knights of St John who erected their cathedral there, named it St John *Colossensis*: does that ring a bell?

I am well aware of not having been able to provide incontrovertible proof, but, as we have all learned from watching television crime series: 'many clues equal proof'.

Who did not live to see the completion of the Colossus was poor old Chares. Tradition has it that he submitted an estimate stating the sum for a statue of half the height of the one actually made. When he was asked to double the height, he merely doubled the estimate, underestimating the cost of the added technical difficulties. Overwhelmed with debts, he committed suicide.

Another tradition has it that the Colossus was paid for out of the sale of the siege machines left behind by Demetrius. It is also likely that the same Helepolis was used as scaffolding.

I have already said that after the earthquake of 228 B.C. its stump and the remnants of the Colossus remained in place for a long time. Pliny tells us that only a very tall man was big enough to put his arm round one finger and Strabo writes that the statue was severed at the knee. It remained there until 653 A.D. when the Saracens sacked the city and appropriated the bronze of the Colossus as well, selling it to a Jewish merchant from Syria who, the chronicles always tell us, transported it to Baghdad with a caravan of 900 camels. There it was converted into pots and pans, thanks to the high percentage of copper in the alloy. Remembering what was said previously about the horses of St Mark's and the increased costs and technical difficulties in using a bronze with a high concentration of copper, we can say that Chares was a worthy pupil of Lysippos and the sky was the financial limit for Rhodes celebrating itself.

So, whoever today would like to take on the mission impossible of tracing a little piece of the bronze of the ancient Colossus will have to take themselves off to the banks of the Tigris or follow the traces of the Mongol tribes of Hulagu, the general of Genghis Khan who sacked Baghdad in 1258 or, even, go to Samarkand, the capital of that Tamerlane who again pillaged Bagdad in 1395. Let us dare to dream; perhaps there is a little piece in your home! By chance have you been to Samarkand and did you buy a copper plate chiselled by a local craftsman?

New York, Liberty Island: The Statue of Liberty

However, there is an easier way to see the Colossus newly erected in all its glory. No, I am obviously not referring to vulgar souvenirs sold in tourist shops or to the even tackier statues that cast a shadow over the aesthetics of the island in various restaurants and hotels. Just as I advised people to go to Agrigento to live the emotion of seeing the Acropolis of Rhodes, I offer a similar piece of advice to those who want to relive the emotion of the Colossus to go to New York and look at the Statue of Liberty.

No, it is not a joke. When Frédéric Auguste Bartholdi conceived the Statue of Liberty, he clearly let himself be inspired by the Colossus, both aesthetically and symbolically. There are notable analogies between the two works of art.

Both are statues of liberty built by peoples who were celebrating a victorious struggle for independence. They were young and strong-minded nations at the beginning of their own journeys to growth and supremacy in their particular world. What had changed were the symbols; for the people of Rhodes, liberty was represented by Apollo Helios, the protective god; for the artist Bartholdi, imbued with the principles of the French Revolution, liberty was female, almost an impersonal goddess of our age. Being a woman, it would have been indelicate for Bartholdi to present her with her legs apart. It was therefore better to cover her with a toga which, incidentally, helped the construction process: a cone rather than the antique tripod.

Both have a clear reference to the sun in the crown of rays which circle the heads of both statues, which, again in both cases, bear a torch. Both look over the sea with the proud mission to be seen at a distance: 'from the sea and the Asiatic continent' the one, 'from twenty-five miles' the other (I should add the caveat 'on a clear day in New York', whereas on Rhodes there is hardly ever this problem). Obviously, the Statue of Liberty is much more imposing; with its 93 metres, including the base, it is almost double the height of the Colossus, but twenty-two centuries of technological progress can hardly have been to no avail.

Even the building techniques are surprisingly similar. Both have an internal structure of stonework, iron and rods. The follower of Chares was that Gustav Eiffel, who was to enjoy undying fame for the eponymous tower in Paris.

Finally, the New York statue is covered with sheets of copper, which is the main ingredient of bronze, the alloy with which the Colossus was covered.

After you have read these lines, I have a question for you: is everything just a figment of my imagination or do you also see significant analogies between the 'iconic monuments' of two epochs, the Hellenistic and ours, with a difference in time of over two thousand years?

And, to conclude, both stand tall, or did stand tall, in the main financial centre of their own time.

The fort of Loryma

Until now, I have told of the 'great' buildings resulting from the construction fever in this century: new walls, the Acropolis, the Colossus. However, let us not forget that Rhodes was recovering from a siege in which it had struggled for its own very survival. It is logical therefore, according to the principle that 'he who has been scalded, also fears cold water', that significant efforts were devoted to military structures as well, and not only to civic ones. The most important testimony to this is the fort of Loryma.

We have already spoken of Peraea and its importance for Rhodes. We have also seen its vulnerability in military terms, being totally surrounded by other states and deprived of 'strategic depth'. Let the proof of this be the speed with which it fell into the hands of Demetrius Poliorcetes, who made precisely this Bay of Loryma his naval base for attacking Rhodes.

Accordingly, the Rhodians decided to construct a protective fort for this part of their own territory. And today it is the structure admired by those boaters eating fish in one of the many tavernas at the water's edge, when they raise their heads. Located on the height which dominates the entry to the inlet, it occupies a rectangular area of 320 by 27 metres. It had eleven towers and five gates and was built of large blocks of stone two and a half metres thick.

The political events of the third century

With the siege over, there were no important political events during many decades. It is incredible how historical narrative likes to concentrate on disasters. I believe that if you asked a thousand people the name of a Roman Emperor who had caught their imagination, nobody would mention Antoninus Pius, and yet the two decades when this emperor reigned were a period of absolute peace and perhaps the apex of material well-being in ancient Rome.

Rhodes experienced something similar in the three generations which followed in the next seventy years: peace and well-being: a fine combination for a good life but one which does not attract historians.

Obviously, a number of things happened and all of them in accordance with the policy of Rhodes to maintain the balance of power and peace to oil the wheels of business. The main events included a slow expansion of Peraea, taking in Stratonikeia to the north and Kaunus to the east with its fertile plane and its harbour, an occasional intervention in its own interests in the Black Sea in favour of the allies Sinope and Byzantium, constant actions against pirates. All of these followed the guidelines set out in the previous chapter.

Peace, and this too is obvious, does not mean self-destructive pacifist demagogy. Sparta, by definition the most 'militaristic' power of Ancient Greece, was also less inclined to let itself be drawn into adventurism. There is nothing more certain that the best way not to be left in peace by some greedy neighbour is to be rich and undefended. Rhodes was rich but always had the good sense to invest heavily in its own defence: walls and a navy. The old Roman adage still holds good: *si vis pacem, para bellum*: loosely translated it means 'If you want to be left in peace, be strong, arm yourself'!

The earthquake of 228 B.C.

For the first significant event, clearly a disaster of the kind historians like, we have to wait for the great earthquake of 228. The city was severely damaged, the Colossus also collapsed. The people reconstructed houses and fortifications, also with the help of other countries concerned, as we have seen, about a possible collapse of the international financial system. The list of donors is extremely long: big and small, rich and poor. Only Attalus of Pergamon is conspicuous by his absence.

As for the Colossus, we have already seen how an oracle protected the wallets of the ancient Rhodians…

Then… 'business as usual'!

Philip V and the First Macedonian War

Unfortunately, the times were ripe for change. In 221 B.C. Philip V ascended to the throne of Macedonia (it's always Macedonia!). When the various historical accounts are taken together, this sovereign appears to us unnecessarily aggressive and ultimately self-destructive, one of those idiots who, whilst harming himself, causes harm to those near to him as well. In this case the nearest of all was Rhodes.

Barely having ascended the throne, the young ruler intervened in the internal disputes of Crete, against Cnossos, the ally of Rhodes. This disturbed the 'divide and rule' policy of Rhodes towards Crete more than a little.

Almost immediately Philip managed to make enemies of the Romans against whom he fought (215/205) the 'First Macedonian War'. If anyone still had doubts about how naïve he was, he should think about this: he knowingly and calculatingly attacked the greatest power of the time! However, the first time, although defeated, he managed to save his bacon; Rome had more important things on its mind, being still busy settling its scores with Hannibal.

The Second Macedonian War

Philip was not to get away so lightly some years later. In 201 B.C., at the Battle of Zama, the Romans defeated Carthage once and for all. The consequence was that, with Carthage, Rhodes lost an important trading partner, but above all, that Rome no longer had any problems in the west and could concentrate all its expansionist policy on the east. As a result, the course of history changed for the Hellenistic world.

With a sense of timing which again reveals a complete lack of foresight, in 202, when Hannibal's fate had been sealed and Rome was about to have its hands free, Philip V again took up hostilities against Rhodes, mainly focusing on its land possessions, whilst also attacking Pergamo.

I have already shown that there was no love lost between Rhodes and King Attalus of Pergamon but, faced with a common enemy, they not only collaborated but decided to ask Rome for help. The Romans arrived and, with the 'Second Macedonian War', supported by its allies Rhodes and Pergamon, definitively defeated Philip in 196.

The Syrian War and the Peace of Apamea

Appetite increases while eating. For Rome it was the turn of the Seleuchid Empire of the king of the day Antiocus III. The war between the Hellenistic ruler and Rome, always supported by Rhodes and Pergamon, lasted from 195 to 188 B.C.. The balance of forces meant that only one outcome was possible. In spite of the support of the military genius Hannibal, Antiocus was defeated and had to sign conditions of peace that amounted to capitulation: 'The Peace of Apamea'. Thanks to this treaty, Rhodes gained some territorial advantages in Anatolia; it was the time of the greatest expansion of Peraea (see the map inserted into Chapter 3 – the control over Peraea and southern Dodecanese).

Rome has arrived

The Peace of Apamea in 188 B.C. is seen by historians as the symbolic moment when the eastern Mediterranean ceased to be governed by a variety of Hellenistic kingdoms forming a balance of power among themselves and became a Roman dominion.

Within this situation, the states of the area had two choices: either align themselves with the wishes of the Eternal City, whatever they were, or be annihilated by it.

This development was devastating for Rhodes; the island lost the freedom of action in foreign policy which had been its fundamental strength in the 'years of glory'.

A new phase in its history opened up. However, before continuing to tell the story, I should like to devote a couple of minutes to a very controversial issue. Given that it was Rhodes which, together with Pergamon, called on Rome to intervene in the eastern Mediterranean, was this the ill-considered act of someone handing over to the hangman the noose which will be used to hang him? In my view, no.

It was exactly the opposite, yet another clear example of *Realpolitik.* Can anyone believe that Rome, with no more enemies in the west, would not have turned its invincible military might towards the rich eastern Mediterranean? Was the mission of Rhodes to the Senate of the Eternal City a turning point or would some other pretext have been used somehow or other by Rome? The answer seems obvious to me. Rhodes therefore did not accelerate its own decline but took note of brutal reality and, as far as possible, it sought to ride the tiger, that is to say jump on to the bandwagon of the incontestable victor, searching at least to reap the relative advantages of being its ally from the very beginning.

To conclude this chapter, I should like to recall that during the 130 years of glory the population increased and the city became a leading cultural centre. However, in order not to break the thread of the narrative artificially, I prefer to recount this aspect organically in the next chapter.

Chapter Five

The slow decline: from 188 B.C. to 44 A.D.

The consequences of Apamea – The quarrels with Lycia and Pergamon – A bride for Perseus – The Third Macedonian War – Rome humiliates Rhodes – A day survived is a day gained – The great school of sculpture: the Winged Victory (Nike) of Samothrace, Laocoön and his Sons, The Farnese Bull and many other masterpieces – Painting and technology – Apollonius of Rhodes – Panaetius – Posidonius of Apamea – Apollonius Molon and Cicero – The Third Punic War and the Mithridatic War – The economic crisis – Rhodes dragged into the civil wars of Rome – 42 B.C.: the sack of Rhodes – The years of the pax augustea and Tiberius at Rhodes – The formalization of the word 'end'

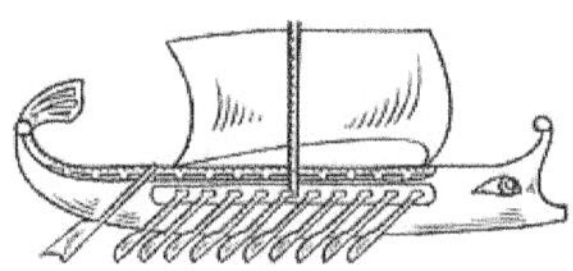

The consequences of Apamea

The political situation resulting from the Peace of Apamea of 188 B.C. is quickly described. Macedonia had already been defeated, Antiochus III of Syria surrendered, Egypt went on being feeble; in fact, Rome could do what it wanted in the eastern Mediterranean. And Rhodes could only take note. Gone forever were the times when it could orchestrate the balance of power.

Rome obviously used its own superiority for its own aims and Rhodes suffered from this. The Italian merchants became ever stronger competitors and enjoyed political support. Even worse was that Rome sponsored the port at Delos which, a duty-free port from 166, became a significant new competitor.

Moreover, Rome interfered in the relations that Rhodes had with the other states: with Pergamon, with the ever-rebellious Lycia, with the Aegean Islands; and this without ever taking any account of the interests of its own little island ally.

On the other hand, Rome did not involve itself in combating piracy (at least not until Pompey did) leaving the whole burden on the shoulders of Rhodes. This, in a context of lower wealth, led to an explosion of tax rates. Many territories and islands broke free from Rhodes asking to be directly dependent on Rome and thus aggravating the problem of the reduction of the tax base. What is more, with the end of Carthage, its most important commercial partner in the area, the economic prospects for Rhodes in the western Mediterranean were destroyed.

Rhodes could only smile and pretend nothing had happened, as it could do nothing else. The alternative would have been that of attracting the vengeance of Rome.

The end of the balance of power was not a case of moral damage, it was much worse. It meant a progressive loss of prosperity. It was a vicious circle. The diminution of prosperity reduced resources for the maintenance of the fleet, which provided the basis for commerce, which, in its turn, was the basis of prosperity, amounting to a negative spiral. The maintenance of the fleet required tax revenues, but in a context of reduced wealth, this implied an increase in the tax rate; the subject territories took their leave reducing the tax base. What could be done? Increase once more the tax rates or decrease the power of the fleet which, however, was the prime instrument for prosperity and therefore the tax base? This, too, represented a downward spiral: there was no rational way out.

Yet it was not yet the end. Of the four and a half centuries of the Maritime Republic of Rhodes, about half were after the Peace of Apamea. Yes, it was a period of decline, but of splendid decline. The city was still very rich and roughly ten generations of the ruling elite were to show themselves capable of not making mistakes, in that they did not accelerate the decline. A level of prosperity was maintained, which, although decreasing, was still enviable.

The priority was, I repeat, not to make mistakes. All the major political choices of this period are easily comprehensible in the light of this guiding principle. Let us examine the main ones.

The quarrels with Lycia and Pergamon

As a result of the Peace of Apamea, Rhodes gained significant territorial advantages, which was some small comfort. Peraea expanded enormously: incorporating to the east all of Lycia, almost as far as the city of Thermessos, upper Antalya. The jewel in the crown was the city of Kaunus with its port and fertile hinterland. To the north Peraea extended to all of Caria up to the Meander River. Formally, some important cities, notably Miletus and Halicarnassus, remained formally independent but tied to Rhodes through a treaty of friendship.

However, the expansion brought problems with it. Caria accepted its new status willingly, whereas Lycia rebelled and Rhodes had to invest energy in subduing it. And yet the problems did not stop there; the Lycians turned to Rome, which, through a Senate jurisconsult, humiliated Rhodes in 178 B.C. stating that, through the Treaty of Apamea, Rhodes had not received Lycia as a gift but as a 'friend and ally'. The difference was not visible on the ground, where Rhodes continued undauntedly its military pressure, but was still enormous. Legally, Rome's interpretation was an alteration of the facts and, politically, a clear slap in the face for its ally. Why was there this gratuitous hostility? As far as Rhodes was concerned, it was for the worst of all reasons. Rome was reminding it, that the island, though being an ally, could not forget who carried the greater clout.

Another problem came from Eumenes, the king of Pergamon. He did his utmost to upset Rhodes. He intervened in the internal affairs of Crete, always strategically important for Rhodes. Then he subjugated the city of Sinope on the Black Sea, a traditional friend that enjoyed the protection of Rhodes. He even supported rebellious Lycia. Rhodes was unable to intervene; it was clear that the Eternal City was on the side of Pergamon. In 172 Eumenes went to Rome and was received with great pomp, very differently from the ambassadors from Rhodes who were there at the same time. Rome was not acting in this way out of sentimentality. Pergamon was the weaker of the two and now the management of the balance of power had passed to Rome, which pursued its own interests.

A bride for Perseus

178 saw a further humiliation of Rhodes by Rome. Perseus, having barely succeeded his father Philip on the Macedonian throne, decided to marry Laodice, the daughter of Seleucus, the king of Syria. However, there was the problem of how the bride might join her future husband. The Treaty of Apamea reciprocally forbade all ships from both countries to enter the waters of the other. Thus, it was a convoy of Rhodes which transported the bride. There was nothing strange in that; to transport people and goods against payment is the everyday business of a ship owner. Furthermore, what reason could there have been for Rhodes to refuse two good customers? It is therefore obvious that the immediate Roman reprimand was totally gratuitous and specious: just another opportunity to show who was the boss.

The Third Macedonian War

The pretext to destroy the last illusions of Rhodes, if it still had any, was the so-called Third Macedonian War fought between 172 and 167 B.C.. Perseus, backed into a corner and with the strength born of desperation, went for broke and declared war on Rome. In fact, in the first four years of the conflict, he enjoyed some success.

Rhodes had to take sides. It was obvious that the heart of everyone was for Macedonia bearing in mind all the gratuitous humiliations inflicted by Rome. Moreover, the fact that Rome had even reduced some Greek citizens to slavery did not attract the sympathy of the Rhodians. However, siding with Macedonia would have been suicidal; reasons of state suggested that it was unwise to go looking for trouble.

Unfortunately, the Assembly was overwhelmingly pro-Macedonia. Perhaps the only case of an institutional change since 396, a new political party was created in opposition to the oligarchs, which came to dominate the assembly. History has told us the names of its leaders: Deinon and Polyaratus.

The result of this was the need for an immense effort by the oligarchs to mediate. This brought into being a policy of compromise, which was fundamentally ambiguous, something that did not escape the Romans.

But what else could the Rhodian leaders have done in face of the pressure of a grumbling population? The presidents of the Prytanes who succeeded each other in turn during these years sent as much aid to Rome as they could, as much as the compromise with the Assembly allowed.

The limit was reached when in 172 they sent six ships (how feeble!) to join the Roman navy commanded by C. Lucretius Gallus. Five of them joined him and the Roman commander sent them back saying he did not need them. He who has ears to hear… The sixth saved a bit of face by taking prisoner the crew of a Macedonian ship it had come across.

Revenge is a dish best eaten cold, and this was well-known in Rome. Thus, as late as the spring 169, a Rhodian delegation was received with full honours. Perhaps this led to an ultimate error of Rhodes. When the fates of war were finally sealed for Perseus, Rhodes tried to save him by proposing mediation. However, on 22

June 168 the Macedonians were routed by the Romans at Pydna, the war was over and the ambassadors from Rhodes, bearers of proposals for peace, were not even allowed into the Roman Senate. A short time later, Perseus was to be paraded through the streets of Rome, chained behind the chariot of victory.

Rome humiliates Rhodes

Now the ball was in the court of Rhodes. Rome asked (in the literal sense of the word) for the heads of the leaders of the pro-Macedonian party, primarily Deinon and Polyaratus. Those who did not commit suicide were executed.

Then the territorial gains acquired through Apamea were revoked, with Rhodes losing Caria and Lycia. This was not yet too serious; things just reverted to how they had been.

Then that status of duty-free port, which I have already mentioned, was conceded to Delos and the island immediately profited from this by creating an image of a port where people 'turned a blind eye', thus immediately taking away from Rhodes all the business 'at the limits of legality', such as the slave trade. But this, too, was not yet fatal for Rhodes; it was precisely the image of somewhere with a trustworthy system that helped it to maintain the key grain business.

What put the system into crisis was the risk of losing 'security', which was fundamental to its own role as a financial centre. Rome knew this well and kept Rhodes in limbo. This was not evil for its own sake, only self-interest. Even the ultra-faithful Eumenius of Pergamon did not receive a much better treatment. Rhodes was on tenterhooks: one inconclusive mission followed the other. Important gifts were sent to Rome, just to beg for a decision, whatever it might be. In the Senate (was it real or a pantomime?) the democratic party of the Gracchus, hostile to Rhodes, and the aristocratic one of Cato, much more favourable to the island, confronted each other.

Finally, the draft of the peace treaty arrived and Rhodes accepted its entirety with a sigh of relief. Indeed, it would have accepted anything just to have certainty. 164 was the year of the formal 'alliance' with Rome, which in reality was an act of submission. It was the end of the substantial independence of Rhodes.

But, once again, what was the alternative? If the Peace of Apamea of 188 had been the beginning of the end, 164 put an end to all doubts even for the most optimistic. Still, realism won out and Rhodes signed.

A day survived is a day gained

From then on, all the policies of the island were based on a struggle to keep the slippery slope leading to its own demise a little less slippery, in keeping with the principle that 'a day survived is a day gained'. However, as we said above, the island was still rich, the commercial and financial spirit remained alive, political harmony reigned. This was the way it was to remain over many generations.

Rhodes then channelled the energies, which it could no longer devote to politics, diplomacy and economic growth, into two centuries of glorious artistic and cultural development, one of the most outstanding the world has ever known. I will interrupt the chronological narrative to illustrate this.

The great school of sculpture: the Winged Victory or Nike of Samothrace, Laocoön and his Sons, The Farnese Bull and many other masterpieces

A rich cosmopolitan metropolis has always attracted scientific, artistic and literary talents, and Rhodes was no exception.

Let us begin with art. I have already spoken about Hippodamus and Dinocrates, as well as of the sculptors Lyssipos and Chares. However, these names in no way comprise the entire list of the members of the great school of sculpture of Rhodes. Not at all! Three of the most famous sculptures of the world were created in the Rhodes of those years: the Nike of Samothrace, Laocoön and his Sons and the Farnese Bull.

When visiting the Louvre, it is impossible not to admire the Nike of Samothrace positioned, with great sense of stage management, in an isolated position at the top of the main stairway of the museum. Moreover, who among us would not be capable of describing from memory this representation of a winged goddess whose arms have been severed by the ravages of time?

We have seen how Rhodes was forced to support Rome in the Syrian War. In particular, a 'Delian League' comprising, among others, Rhodes, Pergamon and Samothrace defeated Antioch III in the naval Battle of Eurymedon in 190. Little is known about this battle, but it is almost certain that the Syrian fleet was commanded by Hannibal himself. Samothrace, a small island in the north of the Aegean, just beyond the mouth of the Dardanelles, decided to celebrate the victory with pomp and constructed the Sanctuary of the Great Gods, also called the 'Cabiri'. Rhodes decided to collaborate donating the main statue: the one that was placed on the highest terrace of this multi-stepped temple. And it was dedicated to the goddess of Victory who in Greek happens to be called 'Nike'.

The Rhodians bought a block of marble from the island of Paros, then considered the most valuable in the world, and entrusted the creation of the statue to their fellow citizen Pythokritos, who represented the goddess with wings and with the right leg posed on the prow of a ship, this sculpted in the grey marble of Lindos.

The Nike is too well-known for it to be worth describing it here, but allow me to add that a fundamental part of its fascination are the missing arms. Successive archaeological expeditions have fruitlessly sought them, and much energy has been extended in imagining how they might have looked. Was the right arm lowered in the act of holding a flagpole, leaning in its turn on the right shoulder? Was the left arm raised to hold a crown? Or? Enigma is a fundamental component of the success of a work of art; what is the smile of the Mona Lisa hiding?

The Laocoon Group

If we move on to the Laocoön group, this was realized in bronze towards the middle of the first century B.C. by three Rhodian sculptors: Agesander and his two sons Athenodoros and Polydorus. The original has been lost, the one conserved in the Vatican Museums in Rome is a very old marble copy; Pliny refers to its presence in the house of Emperor Titus.

It represents an episode in the Aeneid. The priest of Apollo, Laocoön, opposed the entry of the celebrated horse inside the walls of Troy. However, Athena, who desired the success of the Greeks, made serpents rise up from the sea which strangled him together with his sons.

It is the case of one of the most famous sculptures in the world, which had so much influence on art, especially during the Renaissance and Baroque eras. Michelangelo especially expressed all his admiration; art historians profess that some of the works of the great Florentine, such as the Tondo Doni, the Rebellious Slave and the Dying Slave are directly influenced by it.

The third universally famous masterpiece of the Rhodes school of sculpture is the so-called Farnese Bull, the largest sculpture from antiquity ever found and known because of its size as the 'marble mountain'. The version conserved in the National Museum of Naples, is also in this case, an ancient copy accrued from the Farnese collection, hence the name. Its creators were the two Rhodian brothers Apollonius of Tralles and Tauriscus, who lived in the first century B.C. as well. Also in this case, the original was of marble.

The Farnese Bull

As usual, it is Pliny who tells us that the statue was plundered from Rhodes (during the sack of 42 B.C.?). It represents a scene of classical mythology, to which Euripides too dedicated a tragedy: the Punishment of Dirce. Dirce, the queen of Thebes, was killed by the brothers Amphion and Zethus who tied her to a wild bull to avenge their mother, Antiope, ill-treated by the wicked queen Dirce. During the Renaissance some new figures were added to the copy kept at Naples: Antiope herself as well as a child and a dog.

These three are undoubtedly the most notable sculptures of the Rhodes school, but not the only ones. I would flag up to anyone visiting the Archaeological Museum of Rhodes, located in the palazzo built in the fifteenth century by the Knights of St John as a hospital, probably the largest in the world at the time, at least three other unquestionable masterpieces from that time.

First of all, there is a 'Crouching' Aphrodite, found out by Italian scholars in the twenties of the last century. Such a subject is common in classical and Hellenistic Greek sculpture and is represented in the world's most important museums: from the Louvre to Naples, not to mention the Hermitage. The Crouching Aphrodite of Rhodes stands out, being, I believe, the only one of his kind, because of her loose hair, which emphasizes the act of washing.

The second masterpiece is a so called 'Pudica' (chaste) Aphrodite, this also recovered by Italian archaeologists, from the sea opposite the port of Mandraki.

The Crouching Aphrodite

Centuries under the water have not done it any good, but the statue is still very beautiful; the goddess of love and beauty is represented standing and of natural size, slim, with her breasts exposed and wrapped in a twisted sheet, which covers her legs but not her buttocks and pubis (excuse me, why the adjective 'chaste?).

Finally, according to my personal taste, I cannot omit from this list the funeral stele of a woman called Krito, represented together with her pious daughter Timarista.

Painting and technology

Paniting, too, was important in Hellenistic Rhodes, but this form of art is by nature less fortunate than sculpture, being more vulnerable to the ravages of time. No examples of Rhodian painting of that time have survived, only testimonies, of which I will recount two.

The first reveals that, at the beginning of the fourth century, the city commissioned from possibly the most famous living painter, Parrhasius of Ephesus, a friend of Socrates, a group of three knights. We do not know much more.

The second testimony concerns Protogenes, a native of Kaunus but who always lived on Rhodes straddling the fourth and third centuries. We know that he was principally a painter of ships. No work of his has survived, but an anecdote has. Apelles, passing through the island, went to meet him at home and proposed a challenge: who could make a thinner line with a brush. Obviously, Apelles won, but the fact in itself that the great master had paid homage by going to visit him at home and competing with him sounds like eternal homage for our Protogenes.

We have no particular memory of specialists in the world of technology. This is strange. In order to dominate the seas, Rhodes needed great technical capabilities. We know of its excellence in shipbuilding, but - to navigate - astronomy, mathematics and mechanics were also important. We know that those centuries were rich in technical innovation; it is only necessary to think of the 'Antikythera Mechanism', that sophisticated geared machine which precisely calculated the time of sunrise, the lunar phases, the movements of the planets, the equinoxes, all essential components of navigation. We also know of the enormous contribution to technological innovation made in those years by the neighbour Alexandria. Is it possible that Rhodes produced nothing of relevance? From a logical point of view, I would be more inclined to think that there is a lack of sources on our part.

As far as medicine is concerned, the analysis is more logical; Rhodes did not distinguish itself not because it did not invest in this area – it is only necessary to think of the imposing dimensions of the ancient academy of medicine – but because the competition from the all too close Kos, the home of Hippocrates, limited ambitions.

Where Rhodes once more distinguished itself was in literature and philosophy. I have already spoken of the playwrights Antiphanes and Anaxandrides and of the epic poet Peisander, who all left their native Rhodes to make their fortunes in Athens. However, now the times had advanced enough, so not only the sons of Rhodes did not have to emigrate anymore but also Rhodes started attracting foreign talents. Among the many, four have caught my attention: Apollonius of Rhodes,

Panaetius, Posidonius of Apamea and Apollonius Molon. I should like to tell you their stories, in chronological order.

Apollonius of Rhodes

Apollonius of Rhodes, who lived in the third century, was a classic example of the power of attraction exercised by the cultural environment of Rhodes. A native of Egyptian Alexandria, he rapidly became a 'heavyweight'; at the age of only thirty, he became director of the famous Library. However, he quickly came into conflict with his mentor Callimachus, who disapproved of an excessive passion for epic poetry, as well as with his schoolmate Eratosthenes, towards whom he always harboured a deep enmity. A too meteoric career, then as now, if not accompanied by great diplomatic talent, creates a number of enemies who finally crush you. And this perhaps happened to our man, who had to betake himself to Rhodes and there became 'of Rhodes' *par excellence*.

On Rhodes he wrote *The Argonautica*, the only epic to have survived to our time besides those of Homer and Virgil. His pen may not have been equal to that of the two masters, but the subject is fascinating: the great undertaking of the generation of robbers preceding that which sacked Troy. There appear the fathers of the warriors Achilles and Ajax, Peleus and Telamon, then the two twins, one a divine the other mortal, Castor and Pollux, the musician Orpheus, the expedition leader Jason and the helmsman Argo; the perfidious witch Medea and Atalanta, the uncompromising virgin (who knows why?) and the proto-feminist Amazons… It contains an overview of mythological figures everyone has heard of, even if, as an epic poem, it is less known than Homer's and Virgil's poems, perhaps only because it is not part of the school curricula.

Panaetius

After Apollonius of Rhodes it was the turn of Panaetius, a Rhodian of noble birth, who was in his generation, that of the second century B.C., the major exponent of the stoic philosophical school. Panaetius wanted to 'soften' this philosophical movement; for him the aim of life was no longer 'apathy', that is to say the suppression of passions, but disciplining and controlling them. He gave a notable new direction to all the later stoic thinking, some of whose exponents declared their debt to Panaetius, most notably Seneca.

Posidonius of Apamea

However, the greatest legacy which Panaetius left behind was the teaching he gave to his most famous disciple Posidonius, originally from Apamea, but permanently settled on Rhodes, whom many consider the major philosopher of his time, straddling the second and first centuries B.C..

Posidonius was a prolific author with a variety of interests; for this reason, he was called the 'athlete'. He was an all-round genius: a polymath. Rhodian citizenship once acquired, he dedicated himself to politics, being part of delegations to Rome and even president of the Prytaneis. A curious traveller, he described, among other things, the customs of the Celts and their druids.

Interested in science, he studied the tides and was the first person to see a correlation between high water and the phases of the moon. Posidonius was also the first person to engage in measuring the depth of the sea. He constructed a planetarium which reproduced the movement of the stars. He calculated the circumference of the Earth, the size of the moon and its distance from the Earth, as well as the size and distance, always in relation to our planet, of the sun. The figure for the circumference of the Earth, as estimated by Posidonius, was lower than that worked out a century and a half earlier by Eratosthenes of Cyrene, which was closer to the real one and thus, centuries later, Christopher Columbus, who used the calculation of the ancient Rhodian for his voyage to reach India, was somewhat misled.

As a historian, he wrote a 'History after Polybius', taking up where he had left things in 144 and continued it until 85, the year of the victory of Sulla over Mithridates. As a philosopher, his major contribution was about how material prosperity corrupts morals, a recurrent theme in stoic philosophy, and something that he, living during the period of decadence of the Republic of Rhodes, could observe directly. Among those who studied at his school were Pompey the Great and Cicero; the attention paid to him by important later intellectuals, from Seneca to Pliny, from Strabon to Sallust is also most noteworthy.

Apollonius Molon and Cicero

The fourth in my quartet of greats, a little younger than Posidonius, was the rhetorician Apollonius Molon.

Up until that time two schools of oratorical and literary style held sway: the 'Attic' school, so called because it was based on the models of the great Athenian orators of the classical period, such as Lysias, and the 'Asian' school. The Attic School privileged a simple and direct style and its champions in Rome were Licinius Calvus, Junius Brutus and Julius Caesar. By contrast, the Asian School allowed amply for elements of pathos and sentimentality; its champions were Hegesias of Magnesia and, in Rome, the great advocate Quintus Hortensius Hortalus.

Apollonius Molon, who moved to Rhodes from his native Alabanda on the Carian coast, proposed a third way between the two, which, because of him, has passed into history as the 'School of Rhodes', inspired by the style of old Demosthenes. The most famous orator of all times, Marcus Tullius Cicero, was a convinced proponent of this school. Cicero lived in Rhodes between 79 and 77 B.C. specifically to study the rhetoric of Apollonius Molon. Cicero was not the only famous Roman to study rhetoric in Rhodes. To name a few: Julius Caesar and his two murderers, Brutus and Cassius, went there to study.

The Third Punic War and the Mithridatic War

Let us now return to the chronological narrative. After the 'friendship treaty' of 164 B.C., Rome did not feel the need to pile on the agony. What is more it did not need to, since Rhodes, still under the shock of the anxiety it had endured in the months preceding the treaty, was always a model subordinate. When Scipio asked for help in the Third Punic War in 147, Rhodes immediately sent him a strong naval squadron.

Moreover, when in 88 many countries and peoples of the eastern Mediterranean were attracted by the siren voice of Mithridates of Pontus advocating rebellion against Rome, Rhodes took care not to listen, understood immediately that it was a hopeless undertaking and instead helped Rome. At Tenedos in 85, when the Roman general Lucullus won the decisive naval battle against Mithriadates' fleet, Rhodian vessels were part of his fleet and even the flagship itself was from Rhodes.

At the end of the war, the victorious general Sulla recognised the value of this fidelity and gave Rhodes some territories: Kaunus in Lycia, once again, and some Aegean islands.

It should be noted that from Apamea onwards the territorial gains and losses of Rhodes were no longer the result of autonomous political or military actions, but exclusively unilateral steps undertaken by Rome: gains as reward for services rendered or losses for the purposes of punishment. The days of glory were already long gone!

The economic crisis

After 164 B.C. the pace of economic decline accelerated with the loss of Lycia and Caria, even if the latter always remained a faithful ally, removing an important source of taxes. The attempt to collect more revenues by increasing taxation on the islands that were still subject only made

Rhodes lose these as well. They appealed to Rome, whose charges were lower, to allow them to be directly dependent. Clearly, Rhodes was in no position to put up any opposition...

The Kingdom of Pergamon gradually broke away on grain imports passing through the port of Rhodes. Still, the two states had the good sense to stop damaging each other; the fear of offering Rome another *casus belli* in order to intervene was clearly too strong.

In 155 there was more bad news when all the cities of Crete united in a confederation. The traditional strategy of playing them off against one another to fight piracy no longer worked and Rhodes had to increase its own efforts with all the ensuing costs. They also had to confront more or less alone the pirates of the eastern Mediterranean for around eighty years until Rome decided to put an end to the pirates of Cilicia, who had become even more terrifying than those of Crete, and provided Pompey the Great with a strong force to destroy them. It is superfluous to add that Rhodes, this time with enthusiasm, gave ships and men for Pompey's fleet.

We can deduce a clear symptom of the impoverishment in this period from the coinage; since the middle of the first century B.C. the new coins of Rhodes had been minted in bronze and no longer in silver.

Rhodes dragged into the civil wars of Rome

When the long period of Roman civil wars began, Rhodes would have liked to keep out of things, as it could only lose from them. In the context of such civil wars, the position of the island is somewhat reminiscent of the description Manzoni gives of don Abbondio in *The Betrothed*: 'dodge all conflicts and give way in those you cannot avoid; being absolutely forced to take sides between two contenders, choose the stronger, but always have a backstop position and try to let the other party see that you are not wanting to be his enemy'. Rhodes stuck to this as far as possible; these were events which basically did not concern the island.

Thus, in the civil war between Julius Caesar and Pompey (49-45) Rhodes sided with the latter. Besides being a friend from the times of the campaign against the Cilician pirates, he seemed militarily stronger and 'more legitimate', enjoying the support of the Senate but, above all, it would have been very difficult having him as an enemy, since he controlled the eastern Mediterranean.

However, after his defeat at Pharsalus, Rhodes was among the first to leave Pompey's camp and found a way to have itself pardoned by Caesar. A fleet of ten Rhodian ships joined the twenty-five of Caesar in 47 in the 'Battle of the Nile Delta' against the Egyptian rebels. The fleet had to pass through a narrow strait where it risked getting silted up. Caesar hesitated, but not the Rhodian captain, Euphranor, who went ahead with four of his vessels and defeated the Egyptian fleet of a good twenty-two ships. It was the last victorious battle in the history of Rhodes and Euphranor, who died in this battle, was the last in the list of great navarchs of the glorious Maritime Republic.

42 B.C.: The Sack of Rhodes

In 43/42 B.C., after the assassination of Caesar, the choice became much more difficult. Once Rhodes realised that the conspirators were losing, it felt obliged to take up arms to defend itself against them. Marcus Antonius and Octavianus were far away, while Caesar's killer, Cassius, was a neighbour. Cassius, whom, we remember, had been there as a student, intimated surrender and the Rhodians locked themselves inside the walls. However, these were no longer so strong as in 305; with the decline in prosperity the quality of the fortifications, too, had deteriorated. Rhodes surrendered to avoid major trouble.

However, the choice was anything but painless. Cassius executed around fifty leading citizens, but, above all, he stripped the city of its enormous wealth, both public and private: in short, anything that could be moved was stolen. This wealth, among the most substantial in the world, was what had been accumulated in four centuries of successful commercial activity.

Days of raids on homes, public buildings and temples brought Caesar's assassin the incredible sum of 8500 talents, principally in precious metals, and any other object of value, including many objects of art, were carried off. On leaving, Cassius left in the city a garrison of 3000 of his soldiers under the command of Lucius Varo. It was the first time, since the expulsion of the Macedonians in 323, that foreign soldiers stationed inside the walls.

Why did the city, which, 260 years earlier, had resisted victoriously the incommensurably stronger armada of Demetrius Poliorcetes fall like a ripe pear into the hands of Cassius' troops? The answer is already in the question: because now it was a ripe pear. A first consideration is about the military defence capabilities; in 305 Rhodes had won thanks to the walls and the navy. Now decades of subjection to Rome had taken away wealth and therefore any possibility to maintain the walls to their maximum effect, whilst the navy, which no longer ruled the waves, had been much reduced.

It has to be borne in mind that the city was now much bigger, but the majority of the population was foreign. These people were certainly doing well in Rhodes, but they would not have risked their lives to defend it. Just as they had moved from their places of origins to Rhodes, they could have moved a second time. That was the price of multiculturalism.

The third reason was moral. As Posidonius, who had died a few years earlier, had noted, material prosperity corrupts morals. The Rhodians were no longer like their ancestors, who still two and a half centuries previously had the pride of reasserting their Dorian warrior origins as 'sons of Hercules'. The Rhodians of 42 B.C. were the inheritors of centuries of prosperity, of love of culture; they were certainly more 'civilised' but psychologically less motivated and less capable of defending themselves. This seems to me a historical fact; there is always a moment when the rich civilizations succumb under the hammer of more uncouth but more determined peoples.

This was the occasion for the Rhodians to give way to the Romans, but some centuries later it was the turn of Rome to be overwhelmed by the barbarians. To give another example: seeing that I began this book with a parallel between Rhodes and Venice, let us think about the Italy of the Renaissance, perhaps the apogee of wealth and culture of all times for the Boot of Europe. All it needed was a few troops of Charles VIII, descending from France, to make everything collapse like a house of cards. And very quickly, with the loss of independence, there followed the loss of prosperity; as early as 1600 Italy was an economically backward country compared with the rest of western Europe and this was to remain its lot for centuries, only beginning to recover when it regained independence.

If the year 188, thanks to Apamea, was the prologue to the end for Rhodes and if 164, with the friendship treaty with Rome, was the beginning of the end, 42 A.D. was The End tout-court (that with capital 'E'). Thanks to Cassius' marauding soldiers, the intrinsic weakness of the island was fully revealed and the final vestige of independence ceased but, above all, Rhodes lost forever (literally: had taken away from it) wealth accumulated over more than four centuries worth of commerce and finance, which had brought to the island one of the greatest concentrations of movable assets in the world of that time.

At the end of the war, the victorious Antonius rewarded the loyalty of Rhodes by giving it the island of Naxos and some other snippets: very poor business if seen in the light of the stolen riches, but Rhodes was still breathing.

The years of the *Pax Augustea* and Tiberius at Rhodes

Some years later, it all started again. Now it was Caesar's heirs fighting among themselves. Rhodes was with Antonius against Octavianus Augustus for the same reasons as had made it side with Pompey some years earlier: the sense that he was the stronger, traditional good relations and, above all, in order to avoid any repeat of what happened with Cassius. Antonius was its neighbour.

However, when the latter was defeated at Actium in 31 B.C., Augustus took away from Rhodes those few islands which it had received a few years previously from none other than Antonius. Fortunately, the punishment stopped there, he did not wish to pile on more.

From then on, the Mediterranean experienced the *Pax Augustea* and Rhodes had to live under this framework. It was still an important city, pleasant and culturally lively, as is proven by the future Emperor Tiberius, who in 6 B.C., because of disagreements with his stepfather Augustus, chose to remove himself from Rome and retired for seven years into voluntary exile. We remember the sober style of Tiberius, he had an unobtrusive house in the city and a villa outside the walls, and a life very integrated with the local population. The designated successor of the emperor could clearly have taken himself off to any city in the vast Roman world. His decision to go to live in Rhodes offers us an incontrovertible testimony that the ancient republic still radiated an enormous fascination.

The formalization of the word 'end'

Some more years passed until it was 44 A.D., when the decline came to an end. Rhodes lost even the final semblance of independence and was annexed by Rome under Emperor Claudius.

It was, at the same time, the final act in the life of the Maritime Republic and something which we could call a 'non-event'. Claudius closed the eyes of a corpse in the bed: taking note in not a dissimilar way to what centuries later Napoleon did with Venice. And here the parallel I have tried to show between the two maritime republics of Rhodes and Venice reaches its end, like this book.

With 44 A.D. Rhodes ceased to be independent forever. During the remaining period of the Roman Empire, in legal terms Rhodes was the same as so many other Roman cities, even if almost certainly stood out because of its great prosperity; an entrepreneurial culture is neither created nor even destroyed over a few generations.

Thereafter Rhodes followed events, including the disintegration of the Byzantine Empire. Between 1305 and 1522, with the arrival of St John's Knights, Rhodes again experienced a great historical moment. The walls were reconstructed, strong and effective, its ships returned victorious from sweeping the seas; the fight with the growing power of the Turks was for a long time a conflict between equals. However, this is a history of the island of Rhodes not a history of the Rhodians; the glorious Catholic knights all came from western Europe.

Then there followed almost four centuries of relative poverty in the context of somnolent Turkish rule. In the first half of the twentieth century Rhodes enjoyed an enviable period of material and cultural progress, thanks to the Italians that governed the island for some thirty years between 1912 and 1943. Then there were four more years of occupation, equally shared between the Germans and the British. From 1947 onward Rhodes became part of Greece. This leads to the events of our times, when history finishes and becomes chronicle.

Bibliographical Sources and Acknowledgements

When you write a book with the aim of achieving a style accessible to everyone, you are caught between two diverse requirements: on the one hand not to burden the reader with too many references, on the other not to appear superficial in your research. To avoid Scylla and Charybdis, I prefer to give some indication of my sources just once, at this point.

As for the chronicle of the events of the period examined, in addition to the text by Berthold, I found only Rhodes in Ancient Times by Cecil Torr. It is a very old text: it was published in 1885 at the University of Cambridge, but obviously the facts of Hellenistic Rhodes have not changed, and the book is a mine of information: it is difficult to think that even Berthold did not draw on it. The good news, for those wishing to have a more detailed narration of events in ancient Rhodes, is that Torr's book was recently (2005) reprinted by an English publisher.

In relation to archaeological studies, the most important source for this work is the extensive documentation of the archaeological conference 'Rhodes - 2400 years', held on the island in October 1993, but published only in 1999 in Athens, as well as the book The Hellenistic fortifications of Rhodes by Melina Filimonos.

Regarding economic, cultural and artistic life and about the biographies of the 'greats' of Rhodes and the periods preceding and following that examined in this book, the quantity of sources is decidedly asymmetric. Much has been written about the Colossus, any decent history of art book illustrates some of the local masterpieces, such as the 'Nike of Samothrace', 'Laocöon and his Sons' or the 'Farnese Bull'. There are many biographies of important personalities linked to Rhodes, such as Tiberius and Cicero. For almost all of the other people referred to in the book, I have made use of the 'Treccani' encyclopaedia. I have picked up other snippets here and there; for example, I knew the myth of Rhodes rising from the waters, but I also found it in a book by De Crescenzo. I consulted the Iliad and reread the fine book of Kolias on the history of Rhodes during the period of the Knights.

I have realised, once again, how much internet facilitates the work of my generation. Almost all references can be found; obviously they must then be expanded and checked with a great deal of research.

I have probably forgotten some relevant aspect and inevitably I may have let an occasional error slip in. Nevertheless, I hope that I have managed to achieve an outline of the Maritime Republic of Rhodes, which will be seen not only as having a style accessible to everyone but also as being academically correct.

Finally, the thanks. When you write a book for the simple pleasure of doing so, the help from friends plays a fundamental part. Many collaborated in the search for sources, translating texts in languages I do not know well enough, such as Greek and German, and in correcting drafts. Thanks therefore go to Gigi Marengo, Renata Rossi (my mother), David Thompson, Paolo Tomasi and Violanti Vratsanou. A special thanks is due to the researcher of the illustrations, Francesco 'Paco' Lettieri, who, too, loves Rhodes, the island where he has lived for many years. Last but not least, thanks to the translator of the English version, Stuart Parkes.

Chronological Appendix

The background: from the origins to 411 B.C.

Originally	*Zeus raises a mountain from the sea to give it to Apollo, god of the Sun*
10,000 (approx.)	*First presumed presence of human beings on the island*
5,200 (approx.)	*Confirmed beginning of a stable human presence*
15th century	*The Mycenaeans (Indo-Europeans) arrive and merge with the pre-existing Mediterranean population*
13th century	*Rhodes, led by King Tlepolemo, participates in the Trojan War*
XII – IX century	*Greek Dark Ages*
VIII century	*Rhodes re-emerges into history, inserted into the Dorian world. Dorian Hexapolis*
688	*Settlers form Lindos found Gela, in Sicily*
Mid-7th century	*Cleobulus reigns in Lindos for forty years*
582	*Geleans found Agrigento*
490	*Battle of Marathon. The Athenians stop Darius of Persia*

480	*Battle of Salamina. The Greeks definitively defeat the Persians*
431	*The 'Peloponnesian War' begins between Athens and Sparta*
411	*Dorieus, champion of the party of the "oligarchs", takes power in Ialyssos with the Spartan help*

Preparation: from 411 to 323 B.C.

411	*It is decided to build the 'new' city*
408 - 405	*The new city of Rhodes is built*
404	*The Peloponnesian War ends with the victory of Sparta*
396	*In Rhodes, power passes to the party of the 'democrats'. Dorieus is executed in Sparta*
394	*Battle of Cnidus: the Spartan fleet is definitively destroyed by the Persians*
371	*Battle of Leuctra: ephemeral supremacy of Thebes over Greece*
357	*Rhodes rebels against Athens and joins the 'Aegean League'*

338	*Battle of Chaeronea: Philip II imposes the supremacy of Macedonia over all of Greece*
334	*Alexander the Great sets out to conquer the world*
323	*Alexander the Great dies in Babylon*

The days of glory: from 323 to 188 B.C.

323	*Rhodes expels the Macedonian garrison and gains independence*
315	*Antigonus of Macedonia calls on Rhodes to join the alliance against Ptolemy of Egypt. Rhodes gets away with building and selling some ships*
312	*Antigonus again asks for an alliance. Rhodes only provides him with a fleet of ten ships*
306	*Rhodes rejects Antigonus's requests: these are to join in the war against Egypt and to grant access of the Macedonian fleet and soldiers inside the walls of Rhodes*
305 - 304	*The 'Great Siege' of Demetrius "Poliorcetes"*

304 onwards	*Victorious Rhodes builds the "Hellenistic" Walls, the Acropolis, the Colossus and much more (for example, the fort of Loryma)*
293	*The Colossus is finished*
228	*The Great Earthquake. Part of the great destruction, the Colossus collapses*
221	*Philip V becomes king of Macedonia*
215 - 205	*Philip V of Macedonia attacks Rome ('First Macedonian War'), but is defeated*
202 - 196	*'Second Macedonian War'. Rhodes, and Pergamus, are allies of Rome. Macedonia is heavily defeated*
201 (in the meantime)	*In distant Zama, Rome definitively defeats Carthage and can devote all its energies to the Eastern Mediterranean*
195 - 188	*Syriac War. Rome, still having as allies Rhodos and Pergamon, subjugates the Seleuchid kingdom*

190 (in the meantime)	*Battle of Samothrace: the fleet of Rhodes, and with it ships from Pergamon and Samothrace, defeats the Syriac fleet. The Samothracians decide to celebrate it by building a large temple*
188	*Peace of Apamea. Rhodes expands territorially in Peraea, annexing Caria and Lycia*

The slow decline: from 188 B.C. to 44 A.D.

188	*Peace of Apamea. The presence of Rome begins to limit the freedom of action of Rhodes*
178	*Rome makes it clear to Rhodes who is the strongest: jurisconsult of the Senate rules on the relations between the island and Lycia and diplomatic crisis over 'a bride for Perseus'*
172 - 167	*'Third Macedonian War'. While Rhodians are divided over the choice of camp, Rome annihilates Macedonia*
166	*Delos obtains duty-free port status from Rome*

164	*Friendship Treaty with Rome. Rhodes essentially loses its independence*
155	*The cities of Crete cease, after centuries, their internal struggles*
147	*'Third Punic War'. Rhodes sends a naval squadron to help Rome*
88 - 85	*'Mithridatic War'. Rhodes is a faithful ally of Rome and gains some territorial advantages*
49 - 48	*In the civil war between Julius Caesar and Pompey, Rhodes sides with the latter, but is quickly forgiven by the victor*
47	*'Battle of the Nile Delta'. Last great victory of the Rhodian fleet in history*
42	*The 'Sack of Rhodes' by Cassius*
34-31	*In the civil war between Octavianus and Antonius, Rhodes sides with the latter. Octavianus is lenient in his punishment*
6 B.C. 1 A.D.	*The future emperor Tiberius lives in Rhodes*
44 A.D.	*Claudius incorporates Rhodes into the Roman Empire*

Post factum: from 44 A.D. to today

44	*Rhodes is annexed into the Roman Empire*
330	*Emperor Constantine transfers the capital of the Empire to Byzantium (Constantinople). From then on, Rhodes will be a permanent part of the Eastern Roman Empire first and the Byzantine Empire thereafter*
653	*Saracen pirates sack Rhodes. It is one of the many raids suffered, but during this one the ruins of the Colossus are stolen*
1306 - 1522	*Rhodes is ruled by the monastic fighting order of the Knights of St. John and relives part of its ancient splendor*
1523 - 1912	*Ottoman occupation*
1912 - 1943	*Italian occupation. It is a period of economic and cultural rebirth*
1943 - 1947	*German occupation (from 11 September 1943 to 7 May 1945) followed by the British*
1947	*From 23 March, and for the first time in its history, Rhodes becomes part of a Greek national state*

Finished printing
January 2019

Printed in Great Britain
by Amazon

63463728R00112